S0-BCZ-849 014

Ready® Common Core

Mathematics Instruction 3

Curriculum Associates®

Project Manager: Todd Hamer
Revising Editor: Lynn Tauro
Cover Designer and Illustrator: Julia Bourque
Book Design: Scott Hoffman

ISBN 978-0-7609-8638-7
©2014—Curriculum Associates, LLC
North Billerica, MA 01862

No part of this book may be reproduced
by any means without written permission
from the publisher.
All Rights Reserved. Printed in USA.
15 14 13 12 11 10 9 8 7 6 5 4 3

Table of Contents

©Curriculum Associates, LLC   Copying is not permitted.

Table of Contents

©Curriculum Associates, LLC   Copying is not permitted.

Unit 1
Operations and Algebraic Thinking, Part 1

How many 4-ounce bags of carrots will you need to make a salad that calls for 12 ounces of carrots? How many 3-inch blocks will you need to stack to make a 12-inch tall tower? How will you share a box of 12 erasers with 4 classmates?

Sure, you could just guess how many bags of carrots to buy and start handing out erasers until you run out. Or, you could use math facts to help you. $4 \times \underline{\hspace{1cm}} = 12$ and $12 \div \underline{\hspace{1cm}} = 3$ may seem like mysteries at first. But, by learning to make math connections using multiplication and division, you can start to solve these mysteries. These new math connections can be really helpful whether you are sharing erasers, stacking blocks, or making a salad!

✓ Self Check

Before starting this unit, check off the skills you know below. As you complete each lesson, see how many more you can check off!

I can:	Before this unit	After this unit
explain multiplication using equal groups and arrays.	☐	☐
use order and grouping to make multiplying easier, for example: $6 \times 2 \times 5$ is equal to $6 \times (2 \times 5)$.	☐	☐
break apart numbers to make multiplying easier, for example: 3×8 is equal to $(3 \times 4) + (3 \times 4)$.	☐	☐
understand division as a multiplication problem, for example: $10 \div 2$ can be shown as $2 \times \square = 10$.	☐	☐
use the multiplication and division facts up through 10s.	☐	☐
find the rule for a pattern and explain why the pattern works.	☐	☐

©Curriculum Associates, LLC   Copying is not permitted.

Lesson 1   Part 1: Introduction

Understand the Meaning of Multiplication

What is going on when you multiply numbers?

When you **multiply**, you work with equal groups.

These groups of shells are equal.

These groups of shells are not equal.

🔍 **Think** . Multiplication is a way to find how many in all.

When you have equal groups of objects, you can multiply to find a total. This is called **multiplication**.

Each group must have the same number of objects as all the other groups. That's why they are called equal groups.

> **Underline the sentence that tells you what an equal group is.**

There are 3 groups. There are 2 shells in each group.

You can write this as 3×2. 3×2 means "3 groups of 2."

3 groups of 2 shells is 6 shells in all. $3 \times 2 = 6$

©Curriculum Associates, LLC   Copying is not permitted.

🔍 **Think** You can use pictures and models to understand multiplication.

A picture can help you see what multiplication means.

3 groups of 4 balls is 12 balls in all.

$3 \times 4 = 12$ is a multiplication sentence. The numbers you multiply are called **factors**.

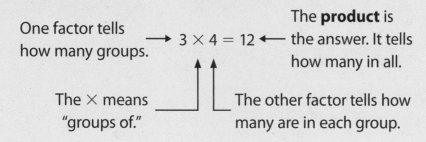

One factor tells how many groups.

→ $3 \times 4 = 12$ ←

The **product** is the answer. It tells how many in all.

The $\times$ means "groups of."

The other factor tells how many are in each group.

When you see $3 \times 4 = 12$, you say, "Three **times** four equals 12."

You can arrange the equal groups into rows and stack them on top of each other. This is called an **array**.

3 rows with 4 balls in each row is 12 balls in all.

$3 \times 4 = 12$

✏️ **Reflect**

1 Do the chairs in your classroom make an array? Explain why or why not.

_____

_____

_____

🔍 Explore It

Using a picture to show equal groups can help you think about multiplication.

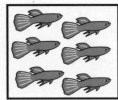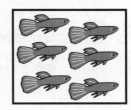

Use the picture to answer questions 2 through 5.

2 How many fish tanks are there? _____

3 How many fish are in each tank? _____

4 How many fish are there altogether? _____

5 What multiplication sentence could you write to tell about the fish? _____

Now try these two problems.

6 There are 4 apple trees in Nell's backyard. She picked 5 apples from each tree. Draw a model to show the equal groups.

7 What multiplication sentence could you write about the apples? _____

©Curriculum Associates, LLC   Copying is not permitted.

💬 Talk About It

Solve the problems below as a group.

8 Look at the picture you drew for problem 6. Explain how you decided what to draw to help you solve the problem.

_____

_____

9 Look at problem 6 again. Draw an array to show the equal groups.

10 Look at the array below.

What multiplication sentence can you write? Explain what each number in the multiplication sentence tells you.

_____

_____

✏️ Try It Another Way

Work with your group to use the rectangles to understand multiplication.

11 You can push the tiles in an array together to make a rectangle. Write the multiplication sentence the rectangle below shows. _____

12 Draw a rectangle made up of square tiles that shows $5 \times 3 = 15$.

🔍 **Connect It**

Talk through these problems as a class, then write your answers below.

13 **Explain:** Travis used the picture below to write the multiplication sentence
    $4 \times 6 = 24$.

What did he do wrong?

_____

_____

14 **Create:** Describe a situation that could be solved using the multiplication
    sentence $9 \times 4 = 36$.

_____

_____

_____

15 **Analyze:** Amelia used the array at right to
    write the multiplication sentence $3 \times 2 = 6$.

    What multiplication sentence would Amelia
    write if she added another row of 2 triangles
    to the bottom of the array?

_____

_____

How would $3 \times 2 = 6$ change if Amelia added 1 more triangle to each row of
the array?

_____

_____

©Curriculum Associates, LLC   Copying is not permitted.

🔍 Put It Together

16 Use what you have learned to complete this task.

> Tucker arranged his pennies in an array.
>
>

A   Write the multiplication sentence the array shows. Explain what each number means.

_____

_____

_____

B   Draw a model to show the multiplication sentence using equal groups.

©Curriculum Associates, LLC   Copying is not permitted.

Lesson 2 Part 1: Introduction

Use Order and Grouping to Multiply

CCSS
3.OA.B.5

In Lesson 1, you learned about the meaning of multiplication. This lesson will help you solve multiplication problems using what you already know. Take a look at this problem.

Ava's mom bought 2 packs of 3 T-shirts. Her dad bought 3 packs of 2 T-shirts. How many T-shirts did each of Ava's parents buy?

Mom   **Dad**

🔍 Explore It

Use the math you already know to solve this problem.

- How many packs of T-shirts did Ava's mom buy? _____

- How many T-shirts were in each of her mom's packs? _____

- What multiplication sentence could you write to find out how many T-shirts Ava's mom bought? _____

- How many packs of T-shirts did Ava's dad buy? _____

- How many T-shirts were in each of her dad's packs? _____

- What multiplication sentence could you write to find out how many T-shirts Ava's dad bought? _____

- Explain what is the same and what is different about the two multiplication sentences you wrote. _____

  _____

  _____

©Curriculum Associates, LLC   Copying is not permitted.

🔍 Find Out More

On the previous page, you saw the order of the factors in a multiplication problem does not matter. If you know that 2×3 is 6, then you also that know 3×2 is 6.

Sometimes you need to multiply 3 numbers together. When that happens, you can use parentheses ( ) to show which two numbers you group together to multiply first.

Jenna bought 4 boxes of hot dogs. Each box has 2 packs. Each pack has 5 hot dogs. How many hot dogs is that?

You can multiply to find the answer like this: $(4 \times 2) \times 5$.

You multiply 4 boxes $\times$ 2 packs in each box. That's 8 packs. Then multiply the 8 packs $\times$ 5 hot dogs in each pack. That's 40 hot dogs.

You can also multiply to find the answer like this: $4 \times (2 \times 5)$.

You multiply 2 packs in each box $\times$ 5 hot dogs in each. That's 10 hot dogs in each box. Then multiply 4 boxes $\times$ 10 hot dogs in each box. Again, it's a total of 40 hot dogs.

✏️ Reflect

1 What did you just learn that can help you with multiplication?

_____

_____

_____

Read the problem below. Then explore different ways to show that the order of factors doesn't matter when you multiply.

Chad read books at the library each week for 6 weeks. He read 3 books each week. Eva read books at the library each week for 3 weeks. She read 6 books each week. Who read more books at the library, Chad or Eva?

🔍 Picture It

You can use equal groups to help you understand the problem.

🔍 Model It

You can also use arrays to help you understand the problem. Each row in the arrays shows the number of books Chad or Eva read each week.

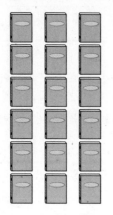

©Curriculum Associates, LLC   Copying is not permitted.

Connect It

Now you will solve the problem from the previous page using equations.

2 What multiplication sentence could you write to find the number of books Chad read? _____

3 What multiplication sentence could you write to find the number of books Eva read? _____

4 Who read more books? _____

5 Explain how you could know that Chad and Eva read the same number of books without finding the product in each multiplication sentence.

_____

_____

_____

6 Your teacher tells you that $8 \times 9 = 72$. Explain how you know what 9×8 equals.

_____

_____

Try It

Use what you just learned about the order of factors to solve these problems.

7 Josie has 5 cups with 4 tokens in each cup. John has 4 cups with 5 tokens in each cup. Draw a model to show that Josie and John have the same number of tokens.

8 Ashish has 6 drawers in his dresser. He puts 8 shirts in each drawer. Asra has 8 drawers in her dresser. If she has the same total number of shirts, how many should she put in each drawer? _____

Read the problem below. Then explore different ways to group factors to help you multiply three numbers.

There are 6 boxes of popsicles in the freezer. In each box there are 4 different colors of popsicles, with 2 popsicles of each color. How many popsicles are in the freezer?

Picture It

You can multiply 6 boxes × 4 colors in each box to find out there are 24 sets of different colors. Then multiply the 24 sets × 2 popsicles of each color.

You could also multiply 4 colors × 2 popsicles of each color to find out there are 8 popsicles in each box. Then multiply 6 boxes × 8 popsicles in each box.

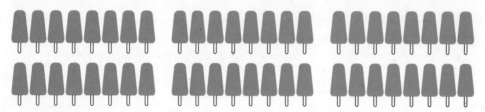

Model It

You can write the multiplication problem and use parentheses to show which two numbers you will multiply first.

$(6 \times 4) \times 2 \longrightarrow 24 \times 2 = 48$

You could also choose to multiply different numbers first.

$6 \times (4 \times 2) \longrightarrow 6 \times 8 = 48$

©Curriculum Associates, LLC   Copying is not permitted.

💡 Connect It

Now you will solve the problem from the previous page using equations.

9 Use parentheses to show one way to group $6 \times 4 \times 2$. _____

10 Use parentheses to show a different way to group $6 \times 4 \times 2$. _____

11 Which way would you pick to solve it? Explain why.

_____

_____

12 Explain how you can use grouping to make multiplying three factors easier.

_____

_____

✏️ Try It

Use what you just learned about grouping factors to solve these problems.

13 Use parentheses to show two different ways to group $7 \times 2 \times 4$. Then choose one of the ways and show the steps to finding the answer.

_____

14 Use parentheses to show two different ways to group $2 \times 4 \times 3$. Then choose one of the ways and show the steps to finding the answer.

_____

©Curriculum Associates, LLC   Copying is not permitted.

Read the problem below. Then explore different ways to order and group numbers to make multiplication easier.

> Joelle bought 2 bags of bananas. There are 9 bunches in each bag, and there are 5 bananas in each bunch. How many bananas did Joelle buy?

🔍 Picture It

Think of the multiplication problem you should write: 2 × 9 × 5.

You can use what you have learned about multiplying in any order and grouping to help make the problem easier.

First, change the order of the numbers. Switch the 2 and the 9.

Now you have 9 × 2 × 5.

Then, group it like this: 9 × (2 × 5).

Multiply the numbers in parentheses: 2 × 5 = 10.

Then do the last multiplication: 9 × 10 = 90.

🔍 Model It

You can use diagrams to help you understand the problem.

The first two diagrams show two ways you can solve the problem using just grouping. The third diagram shows how you can solve the problem by changing the order of the numbers before using grouping.

```
  2 × 9 × 5          2 × 9 × 5          9 × 2 × 5
   \ /  |             |  \ /             |  \ /
   18 × 5             2 × 45            9 × 10
     \  /              \  /              \  /
      90                90                90
```

©Curriculum Associates, LLC　Copying is not permitted.

Connect It

Now you will choose which way to solve the problem from the previous page.

15 You can order and group the factors in the multiplication sentence $2 \times 9 \times 5$ in different ways. Look at some of them shown below. Fill in the missing numbers.

$(9 \times 2) \times$ _____ $= 90$ $(5 \times 2) \times$ _____ $= 90$ _____ $\times (9 \times 5) = 90$

16 Remember that you must multiply numbers inside parentheses first. Look back at the problems in question 15. Multiply the numbers in the parentheses, then fill in the missing numbers below.

(_____) $\times$ _____ $= 90$ (_____) $\times$ _____ $= 90$ _____ $\times$ (_____) $= 90$

17 Which of these three multiplication sentences do you think is the easiest to solve? Explain why you think so.

_____

_____

18 Explain how you can use grouping and multiplying in any order to make multiplying three numbers easier.

_____

_____

Try It

Use what you just learned about ordering and grouping factors to solve these problems.

19 Change the order and use parentheses to show one way to solve $3 \times 7 \times 3$. Then show the steps to finding the answer.

_____

20 Change the order and use parentheses to show one way to solve $4 \times 9 \times 2$. Then show the steps to finding the answer.

_____

Study the model below. Then solve problems 21–23.

The first array shows 5 × 8. The second array looks the same, just turned on its side. It shows 8 × 5.

Student Model

There are 8 rows of tables in the cafeteria. Each row has 5 tables. Maria knows that 5 × 8 is 40. How can she use this to figure out how many tables there are?

Look at how you could show your work using arrays.

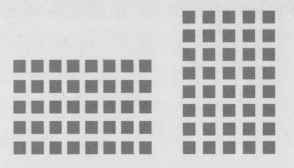

Solution: __You can multiply numbers in any order.__

__5 × 8 = 40, so 8 × 5 = 40. There are 40 tables.__

Pair/Share

If two arrays have the same total, how do they show two different multiplication facts?

Which two numbers have a product that would be easy to multiply by in your head?

21 There are 2 classes of third graders. In each class, there are 3 rows of desks, with 7 desks in each row. Write the multiplication sentence and show how to group so that it is easiest to figure out the number of desks in both classes. Then find the answer.

Show your work.

Pair/Share

How would solving the problem be different if you grouped it another way?

Solution: _____

©Curriculum Associates, LLC   Copying is not permitted.

22 AJ needs to solve $3 \times 8 \times 2$. Show one way to find the answer. Use parentheses to show how you grouped the numbers.

Show your work.

I think it would be easiest if you changed the order of the factors before you grouped them.

Solution: _____

Pair/Share

How did you decide which two numbers to multiply first?

23 Matt knows $4 \times 6 = 24$. What other math fact does this help Matt remember? Circle the letter of the correct answer.

A $6 + 4 = 10$

B $8 \times 3 = 24$

C $24 - 6 = 18$

D $6 \times 4 = 24$

Sadie chose A as the correct answer. How did she get that answer?

_____

_____

What have you learned about the order of factors in multiplication?

Pair/Share

Does Sadie's answer make sense?

©Curriculum Associates, LLC   Copying is not permitted.

Solve the problems.

1   Jackson knows $9 \times 7 = 63$. He needs to solve _____ $\times\ 9 = 63$. What number goes in the blank?

    A   5

    B   6

    C   7

    D   8

2   Which of the following is NOT true?

    A $3 \times 6 \times 3 = 6 \times 3 \times 3$

    B $3 \times 6 \times 3 = 9 \times 3$

    C $3 \times 6 \times 3 = 9 \times 6$

    D $3 \times 6 \times 3 = 3 \times 18$

3   Emma's service group is making sandwiches for a community picnic. There are 7 children in the service group. Each child is making 5 sandwiches. It takes 2 slices of bread to make a sandwich. What is the total number of slices of bread the children need to make the sandwiches?

    _____

©Curriculum Associates, LLC   Copying is not permitted.

4 Lyn's mom has pictures arranged on her refrigerator in rows. There are 3 rows of pictures. There are 7 pictures in each row. Which of the following expressions or arrays could be used to find the total number of pictures? Circle the letter for all that apply.

A 3×7

B 7×3

C $7 \times 7 \times 7$

D
□□□
□□□
□□□
□□□
□□□
□□□
□□□

E
□□□□□□□
□□□□□□□
□□□□□□□

5 Dan has 2 photo albums. Each photo album has 8 pages. Dan can fit 4 pictures on each page. How many pictures can Dan fit in the albums?

Show your work.

Answer _____ pictures

✓ **Self Check** *Go back and see what you can check off on the Self Check on page 1.*

Lesson 3   Part 1: Introduction 👥

Split Numbers to Multiply

In Lesson 2, you learned some ways to make multiplying numbers easier. Take a look at this problem.

Ty has 5 bunches of carrots. There are 3 carrots in each bunch. How many carrots does Ty have altogether?

🔍 Explore It

Use the math you already know to solve the problem.

- Circle 4 of the bunches. What multiplication problem can you write to find how many carrots are in 4 bunches? _____

- Circle the 1 bunch that is left. What multiplication problem can you write to find how many carrots are in 1 bunch? _____

- Explain how you could use the two sets of bunches you circled to find the total number of carrots.

  _____

  _____

  _____

©Curriculum Associates, LLC   Copying is not permitted.

🔍 Find Out More

You can break apart numbers to help you figure out multiplication problems you do not know.

Ty did not know what 5 groups of 3 were, but he did know what 4 groups of 3 were. That left 1 group of 3.

Ty broke apart 5 into $4 + 1$. Then he multiplied each part by 3 and added the products together.

You can write 4 bunches of 3 carrots plus 1 bunch of 3 carrots like this:
$(4 \times 3) + (1 \times 3)$

The parentheses show you that you multiply each set of numbers first, and then add them together.

You can also show this using an array.

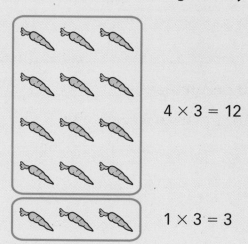

$4 \times 3 = 12$

$1 \times 3 = 3$

You can write it three ways: 5×3 or $(4 + 1) \times 3$ or $(4 \times 3) + (1 \times 3)$

✏️ Reflect

1 What if Ty had 4 carrots in each bunch instead of 3? Explain how he could break apart the numbers to find the answer to 5×4.

_____

_____

_____

Read the problem below. Then explore different ways to break apart one of the numbers to solve the problem.

> Mario has 6 vases of flowers. There are 4 flowers in each vase. How many flowers does Mario have in all? Break apart one of the numbers to find the answer.

🔍 Picture It

You can use equal groups to help understand the problem.

Mario chose to break apart the number of groups to find the answer.

🔍 Model It

You can also use an array to help understand the problem.

Mario made an array and then broke apart the rows to show the new groups.

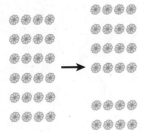 

🔍 Solve It

You can also use words to help understand the problem.

6 vases of 4 flowers is the same as 4 vases of 4 flowers plus 2 vases of 4 flowers.

💡 Connect It

Now you will explore different ways to solve the problem from the previous page.

2 What numbers did Mario break 6 into to help him solve the problem?

_____

3 What two smaller multiplication facts did Mario solve?

_____

4 What is another way you could break apart 6 to solve the problem 6 × 4?

_____

5 What numbers could Mario break 4 into to help him solve the problem?

_____

6 What two smaller multiplication facts would Mario solve if he broke apart the 4?

_____

7 Explain why Mario's way of solving the problem is not the only way.

_____

_____

✏️ Try It

Use what you just learned to solve this problem.

8 Show two different ways to break apart the numbers to solve 4 × 3. Draw models and show the math problems you used.

_____

_____

Read the problem below. Then explore ways to break apart a number to make one hard multiplication sentence into two easier multiplication sentences.

> Matt shared some crackers with 8 friends. He gave each friend 7 crackers. How many crackers did Matt give away? Break apart one of the numbers to find the answer.

Model It

You can use an array to help understand the problem.

Instead of breaking apart the rows (the number of friends), Matt broke apart the columns (the number of crackers).

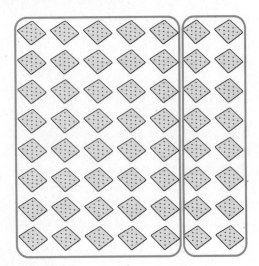

Solve It

You can also use words and equations to help understand the problem.

Giving 8 friends 7 crackers is the same as giving 8 friends 5 crackers each, then giving each of them 2 more crackers. You can write it three ways:

$$8 \times 7 \quad \text{or} \quad 8 \times (5 + 2) \quad \text{or} \quad (8 \times 5) + (8 \times 2)$$

©Curriculum Associates, LLC   Copying is not permitted.

Connect It

Now you will think more about the problem from the previous page.

9 What numbers did Matt break 7 into to help him solve the problem? _____

10 What two smaller multiplication problems did Matt solve? _____

11 Show how to use the two multiplication problems to find the answer.

_____

12 Madison knows the answer to 4×7. How can this help her multiply 8×7?

_____

_____

13 Explain why someone might want to break apart one of the numbers in a multiplication problem.

_____

_____

Try It

Use what you learned about breaking apart numbers to solve these problems.

14 Alice knows the answer to 5×7. How can that help her find the answer to 6×7? Draw a model and show the math problems you used.

_____

15 Tim knows the answer to 6×7. How can that help him find the answer to 6×9? Draw a model and show the math problems you used.

_____

Study the model below. Then solve problems 16–18.

Student Model

The student broke apart the 4 into 2 + 2 and then added the two products together.

Stacy is making 4 bracelets. Each bracelet uses 7 silver beads. How many silver beads does Stacy need? Show how to break apart one of the numbers to make the problem easier to solve.

Look at how you could show your work using an array.

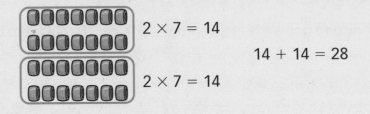

$2 \times 7 = 14$

$14 + 14 = 28$

$2 \times 7 = 14$

Solution: __28 silver beads__

💬 Pair/Share

How else could you have broken apart one of the numbers to solve this problem?

---

16 There are 6 bowls of apples. There are 6 apples in each bowl. Show how to break apart one of the numbers to make the problem easier to solve.

What multiplication problem using 6 has an answer that would be easy to add to another number?

💬 Pair/Share

What is another model you could have used to show how to break the problem apart?

©Curriculum Associates, LLC   Copying is not permitted.

17 Joe has 8 shelves with 9 books on each shelf. How many books does Joe have altogether? Show how to break apart one of the numbers to make the problem easier to solve.

You can use many different ways to "break apart" a 9.

Solution: _____

Pair/Share

How did you and your partner decide how to break apart one of the numbers?

18 Jordan solved 6 × 8 by breaking apart the 6 into 5 + 1. Which of the following correctly shows the next step in finding the solution? Circle the letter of the correct answer.

A (5 × 6) + (1 × 6)

B (6 × 8) + (1 × 8)

C (5 + 8) × (1 + 8)

D (5 × 8) + (1 × 8)

Avery chose A as the correct answer. How did she get that answer?

What smaller multiplication problems did Jordan solve?

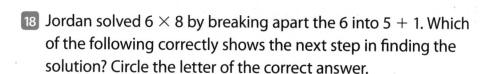

Pair/Share

Does Avery's answer make sense?

Solve the problems.

1 Tucker solved 7 × 5 by breaking it apart as shown below.

(7 × 3) + (7 × _____)

What number should go in the blank?

A 1

B 2

C 4

D 8

2 Cole has 8 packs of pencils. There are 5 pencils in each pack. He solved the problem by breaking it apart using the model below.

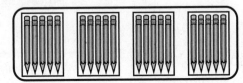 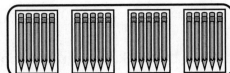

Which shows how Cole solved the problem?

A (4 × 5) + (4 × 5)

B (8 × 2) + (8 × 2)

C (4 × 2) + (4 × 2)

D (3 × 5) + (5 × 5)

©Curriculum Associates, LLC   Copying is not permitted.

3 Use the array below to solve 8 × 8. First draw circles to break the array into two groups. Then fill in the blanks to show how you broke the numbers apart.

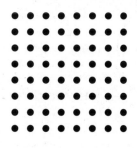

$$8 \times 8 = (8 \times \underline{\quad}) + (8 \times \underline{\quad})$$

4 For each expression in 4a–4e, answer *Yes* or *No* if the expression is equivalent to the product of 6 and 9.

a. (6 × 3) + (6 × 3) ☐ Yes ☐ No

b. (6 × 4) + (6 × 5) ☐ Yes ☐ No

c. 6 × (6 + 3) ☐ Yes ☐ No

d. 9 × (2 + 4) ☐ Yes ☐ No

e. (9 × 3) + (9 × 3) ☐ Yes ☐ No

5 There are 9 rows in Mrs. Mitchell's flower garden. Each row has 9 flowers planted in it. How many flowers are planted in the garden? Show how to break apart the numbers to find the answer.

Answer There are _____ flowers in the garden.

✓ **Self Check** *Go back and see what you can check off on the Self Check on page 1.*

©Curriculum Associates, LLC   Copying is not permitted.

Lesson 4   Part 1: Introduction 👥

Understand the Meaning of Division

CCSS
3.OA.A.2

> **What is going on when we divide numbers?**

Division does exactly what it says—it lets you divide. It lets you take a total and break it up into groups.

When you divide, you must put the same number in each group.

Suppose you have a total of 6 socks. One way you can divide the socks is to make 3 groups and put 2 socks in each group.

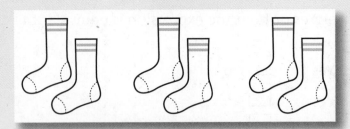

There are 6 socks in all. There are 3 groups. There are 2 socks in each group.

🔍 **Think** You can use division to find the number in each group.

When you know the total and the number of groups, you can divide to find how many to put in each group.

Circle the division sentence.

Jake has 8 cookies and 2 plates. He puts the same number of cookies on each plate.

divided into

There are 8 cookies in all. There are 2 groups.

$8 \div 2$ tells you how many cookies Jake puts on each plate.

There are 4 cookies on each plate.

$8 \div 2 = 4$

©Curriculum Associates, LLC   Copying is not permitted.

🔍 **Think** You can use division to find the number of groups.

When you know the total and the number in each group, you can divide to find how many groups you can make.

Missy has 15 balloons. She ties them into groups of 3.

15 ÷ 3 tells you how many groups Missy can make.

Did you notice that a division sentence always starts with the total amount?

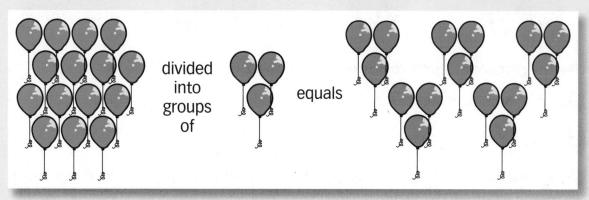

divided into groups of   equals

There are 15 balloons in all. There are 3 balloons in each group.

There are 5 groups of balloons.

15 ÷ 3 = 5

✏️ **Reflect**

1 Use your own words to explain how drawing a picture can help you solve a division problem.

_____

_____

_____

_____

©Curriculum Associates, LLC   Copying is not permitted.

🔍 Explore It

Using a model to show equal groups can help you think about division.

Use the picture of shells to answer questions 2 through 5.

2 How many shells are there? _____

3 How many pails are there? _____

4 Ben wants to put the same number of shells in each of the pails. How many shells should he put in each pail? _____

5 What division sentence could you write to tell about the shells? _____

Now try these two problems.

6 Marc's dad picked 24 oranges. He wants to put all the oranges in bags. He decides to put 6 oranges in each bag. Draw a model to show how many bags he needs.

7 What division sentence could you write about the oranges? _____

©Curriculum Associates, LLC   Copying is not permitted.

💬 Talk About It

Solve the problems below as a group.

8 Look at the picture you drew for problem 6. Explain how you decided what to draw to help you solve the problem.

_____

_____

9 Look at problem 6 again. Imagine Marc's dad changes his mind. Instead of putting 6 oranges in each bag, he decides to put all the oranges in 6 bags. He will put the same number of oranges in each bag. How does this change the division in problem 6?

_____

_____

10 Draw a picture to show the new situation.

✏️ Try It Another Way

Work with your group to use the arrays to solve the division sentences.

11 $45 \div 5 =$ _____

12 $42 \div 7 =$ _____

©Curriculum Associates, LLC   Copying is not permitted.

🔍 Connect It

Talk through these problems as a class, then write your answers below.

13 Explain: Maddy used this array of stars to show the division problem 8 ÷ 4 = 2.

What did she do wrong?

_____

_____

14 Create: Describe a situation that could be solved using the division problem 16 ÷ 2 = 8.

_____

_____

15 Compare: David and Mitch each bought a bag of pears at the grocery store. Look at how each boy divided his pears into equal groups.

David

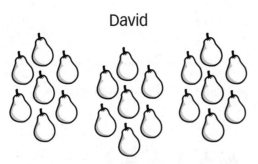

Mitch

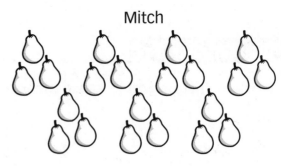

What is the same about the two bags of pears?

_____

_____

What is different about the two bags of pears?

_____

_____

©Curriculum Associates, LLC   Copying is not permitted.

Put It Together

16 Use what you have learned to complete this task.

> Cory has 20 crayons. He wants to give the same number of crayons to each of his friends.

A Write two different questions about Cory's crayons that can be answered using division.

1. _____

_____

_____

2. _____

_____

_____

B Choose one question to answer. Circle the number of the question you chose. Show how to find the answer using pictures or an array. Then write the division sentence that shows the answer to your question.

_____

_____

_____

©Curriculum Associates, LLC   Copying is not permitted.

Lesson 5   Part 1: Introduction

Understand How Multiplication and Division Are Connected

> **How are multiplication and division related to each other?**

Multiplication joins equal groups to find a total. The answer is called the product. Division starts with a total and breaks it up into equal groups. The answer is called the quotient.

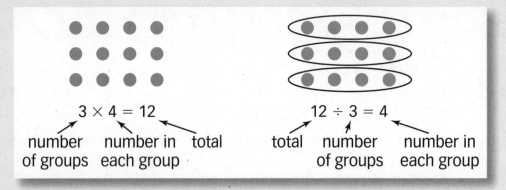

$3 \times 4 = 12$

number of groups   number in each group   total

$12 \div 3 = 4$

total   number of groups   number in each group

🔍 **Think**   You can use multiplication or division number sentences to describe a problem.

Circle the total in each number sentence.

Juan arranges some pennies in an array.

You can use multiplication to tell how many pennies in all.

$4 \times 8 = 32$ pennies   or $8 \times 4 = 32$ pennies

You can use division to tell how many pennies are in each row and how many rows there are.

$32 \div 4 = 8$ pennies in each row   or $32 \div 8 = 4$ rows of pennies

Notice that all of the equations use the same three numbers.

©Curriculum Associates, LLC   Copying is not permitted.

🔍 **Think** Division equations have related multiplication equations.

To help you solve a division problem, you can write a multiplication equation and find the unknown number.

Nina buys 20 stickers. She puts the same number of stickers on each of 5 pages in her scrapbook. How many stickers does she put on each page?

5 times what number equals 20?

You know the total (20 stickers) and the number of groups (5 pages). What you need to find is the number in each group. In other words, it is the number of stickers on each scrapbook page.

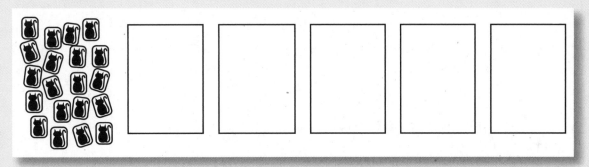

A division equation for the problem is

$20 \div 5 = \boxed{}$

$20 \div 5 = \textbf{4}$

A multiplication equation for the problem is

$5 \times \boxed{} = 20$

$5 \times \textbf{4} = 20$

Nina puts 4 stickers on each page.

Now you'll have a chance to solve problems using the relationship between multiplication and division.

✏️ **Reflect**

1 Use your own words to explain how you could use multiplication to find $35 \div 5$.

_____

_____

Explore It

You can think about a problem as division or multiplication.

Read the following problem. Then answer questions 2 through 5.

A pet store has 18 hamsters. The shop owner wants to put 3 hamsters in each cage. How many cages does the shop owner need for all the hamsters?

2 Draw a model using equal groups or an array to show the problem.

3 Write a division equation for the problem. Use a ☐ for the unknown number.

_____

4 Write a multiplication equation for the problem. Use a ☐ for the unknown number.

_____

5 How many cages does the shop owner need? _____

Now read this problem and answer questions 6 through 8.

Manuel has 42 quarters. He puts them into 7 piles. He puts the same number of quarters in each pile. How many quarters are in each pile?

6 Write a division equation for the problem. Use a ☐ for the unknown number.

_____

7 Write a multiplication equation for the problem. Use a ☐ for the unknown number.

_____

8 How many quarters are in each pile? _____

©Curriculum Associates, LLC   Copying is not permitted.

💬 Talk About It

Solve the problems below as a group.

9 Look at your answer to problem 6. Explain how you knew what equation to write.

_____

_____

Look at your answer to problem 7. How can you use your multiplication equation to solve the problem?

_____

_____

10 Justin knows that $8 \times 7 = 56$. What division problems can he answer?

_____

_____

✏️ Try It Another Way

Work with your group to find the number that goes in the ☐ for each problem below.

11 $3 \times \boxed{} = 24$

$24 \div 3 = \boxed{}$ $\boxed{} =$ _____

12 $\boxed{} \times 9 = 54$

$54 \div \boxed{} = 9$ $\boxed{} =$ _____

Connect It

Talk through these problems as a class, then write your answers below.

13 **Identify:** Elisa planted the same number of flowers in each pot. Look at the picture below. Then write two multiplication and two division equations that the picture shows.

_____

_____

14 **Explain:** Yasmin saw the problem $63 ÷ \boxed{} = 7$ and thought, "There are 63 things in all that are divided into groups. There are 7 in each group." Explain how Yasmin can use multiplication to help her find the number of groups.

_____

_____

15 **Analyze:** Marissa has 4 boxes of markers with 6 markers in each box. She wrote the following equations:

$4 \times 6 = 24$

$6 \times 4 = 24$

$24 ÷ 4 = 6$

$24 ÷ 6 = 4$

Circle the number in each equation that shows the total number of markers.
Put a box around the number in each equation that shows the number of groups.
Underline the number in each equation that shows the number in each group.

©Curriculum Associates, LLC   Copying is not permitted.

Put It Together

16 Use what you have learned to complete this task.

   A Write a word problem about arranging desks in a classroom that can be solved using the equation $5 \times \boxed{} = 15$.

   _____

   _____

   _____

   B Solve your problem. Draw a model that shows your problem and solution.

Lesson 6   Part 1: Introduction

CCSS
3.OA.A.4
3.OA.C.7

Multiplication and Division Facts

You understand that multiplication and division are related. Look at this problem to see how this can help you work with division facts.

> Kenny has 24 marbles. He puts the same number of marbles into each of 3 bags. How many marbles are in each bag?

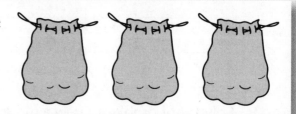

Explore It

Use math you already know to solve the problem.

- Write the division problem you need to solve to answer this question. _____

- Think about this as a multiplication problem.
  How many equal groups are there? _____

- You don't know how many marbles are in each group. How can you write a

  multiplication fact that says 3 groups of ☐ marbles is 24? _____

- Here are multiplication facts for 3.
  Write the one that matches this problem. _____

$3 \times 1 = 3$	$3 \times 3 = 9$	$3 \times 5 = 15$	$3 \times 7 = 21$	$3 \times 9 = 27$
$3 \times 2 = 6$	$3 \times 4 = 12$	$3 \times 6 = 18$	$3 \times 8 = 24$	$3 \times 10 = 30$

- What number is ☐? _____

- How many marbles are in each bag? _____

- How could you check your answer?

  _____

  _____

  _____

©Curriculum Associates, LLC   Copying is not permitted.

🔍 Find Out More

Fact families are sets of related multiplication and division facts. Here is one example:

$3 \times 8 = 24$ $8 \times 3 = 24$ $24 \div 8 = 3$ $24 \div 3 = 8$

This shows two multiplication facts and two division facts. All the facts use the same three numbers. If you know one fact in the family, then you can find all the others, too.

When you are solving multiplication or division problems, the number that you don't know might be any one of the three numbers in a fact family. You can choose any fact in the family to help you think about the answer.

For example, you might write the fact $6 = \boxed{} \div 9$ to solve a problem. Here is the whole fact family:

$\boxed{} \div 6 = 9$ $\boxed{} \div 9 = 6$ $6 \times 9 = \boxed{}$ $9 \times 6 = \boxed{}$

Here is an array that shows the numbers in this fact family.

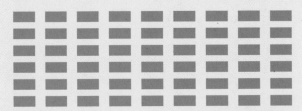

The array shows that 6×9 and 9×6 are both equal to 54. If you know one of the multiplication facts, you can complete the division facts: $54 \div 6 = 9$ or $54 \div 9 = 6$.

✏️ Reflect

1 How are the multiplication facts in a fact family alike? How are they different? How are the division facts alike and different?

_____

_____

_____

Read the problem below. Then explore different ways to find a division fact answer.

Jo knows nickels are worth 5 cents, and she needs 40 cents altogether. She wants to find out how many nickels she needs. Jo writes 40 ÷ 5 = ☐.

Picture It

You can use a number line to help you understand the problem.

Skip count by 5s to find the answer. Start at 0 and jump by 5s until you get to 40.

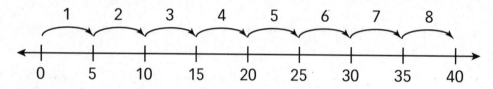

Model It

You can use fact families and multiplication facts you know.

Here are the facts in this family:

$5 \times \boxed{} = 40$ $\boxed{} \times 5 = 40$ $40 \div \boxed{} = 5$ $40 \div 5 = \boxed{}$

Write the multiplication facts for 5:

5 × 1 = 5	5 × 3 = 15	5 × 5 = 25	5 × 7 = 35	5 × 9 = 45
5 × 2 = 10	5 × 4 = 20	5 × 6 = 30	5 × 8 = 40	5 × 10 = 50

Look for the fact that uses the same numbers. Use that fact to fill in the blanks in the fact family.

©Curriculum Associates, LLC   Copying is not permitted.

Connect It

Now you will use fact families to solve another problem like the one on the previous page.

2 Mo wants to know how many nickels he needs to make 45 cents. He writes $45 \div \boxed{} = 5$. What other division fact can he write to model this problem?

_____

3 What two multiplication facts are in the same fact family? Write multiplication facts with unknowns.

_____

4 Look at the list of multiplication facts for 5 on the previous page. Which fact will help Mo answer his division problem? _____

5 Explain how you know which multiplication fact you can use to help you find any division fact.

_____

_____

_____

Try It

Use what you just learned about fact families and the relationship between multiplication and division to solve these problems.

6 Write the missing product. Then complete this fact family.

$2 \times 3 = \boxed{}$ _____ _____ _____

7 Write two multiplication facts Brice can use to solve $\boxed{} \div 3 = 7$.

_____

_____

©Curriculum Associates, LLC   Copying is not permitted.

Read the problems below. Then explore different ways to use a multiplication table to solve multiplication and division problems.

Find the missing numbers.

$2 \times$ ____ $= 10$ $24 \div 6 =$ ____ $6 \times$ ____ $= 48$ ____ $\div 9 = 8$

 Picture It

You can use a multiplication table to solve multiplication and division problems.

A multiplication table shows all of the multiplication and division facts.

	0	1	2	3	4	5	6	7	8	9
0	0	0	0	0	0	0	0	0	0	0
1	0	1	2	3	4	5	6	7	8	9
2	0	2	4	6	8	10	12	14	16	18
3	0	3	6	9	12	15	18	21	24	27
4	0	4	8	12	16	20	24	28	32	36
5	0	5	10	15	20	25	30	35	40	45
6	0	6	12	18	24	30	36	42	48	54
7	0	7	14	21	28	35	42	49	56	63
8	0	8	16	24	32	40	48	56	64	72
9	0	9	18	27	36	45	54	63	72	81

Model It

Use the table above to complete the fact family.

The multiplication table shows the three numbers that belong in a fact family. Look at the row for 2. Go across to find 10. Then look up that column to find the third number in the fact family. Then fill in the blanks in the fact family.

$2 \times$ ____ $= 10$ $10 \div 2 =$ ____

____ $\times 2 = 10$ $10 \div$ ____ $= 2$

©Curriculum Associates, LLC   Copying is not permitted.

Connect It

Now you will use the multiplication table to find the answers to the other three problems.

8 Look at the multiplication table. What are the three numbers in the fact family for

24 ÷ 6 = _____ ? _____

Now fill in the blank: 24 ÷ 6 = _____

9 What are the three numbers in the fact family for 6 × _____ = 48? _____

Now fill in the blank: 6 × _____ = 48

10 What are the three numbers in the fact family for _____ ÷ 9 = 8? _____

Fill in the blank: _____ ÷ 9 = 8

11 Explain how you can use a multiplication table to find the 3 numbers in any fact family.

_____

_____

_____

Try It

Use what you just learned about using a multiplication table to solve these problems.

12 Use the multiplication table to write the equations in the fact family that includes 42 and 6.

_____

13 Fill in the missing number: 56 ÷ _____ = 8

©Curriculum Associates, LLC   Copying is not permitted.

Study the model below. Then solve problems 14–16.

Student Model

Today some students will give an oral report. The teacher has planned 15 minutes for all the reports. Each student gets 3 minutes. How many students are giving reports?

Solve $3 \times \boxed{} = 15$

Look at how you could show your work using a number line.

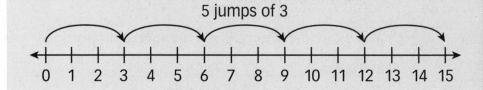

5 jumps of 3

0 1 2 3 4 5 6 7 8 9 10 11 12 13 14 15

Solution: __5 students__

Each jump on the number line stands for 1 student.

Pair/Share

What other equations can be used to solve this problem?

14 There are 35 students in the math club. They break into groups of 5 to work on a project. How many groups are there?

Solve $35 \div \boxed{} = 5.$

How can you find the third number in this fact family?

Pair/Share

What are the other facts that belong to this fact family?

Solution: _____

©Curriculum Associates, LLC   Copying is not permitted.

15 Each package contains 4 party favors. Sheila buys 9 packages. How many party favors does she buy? Solve $4 \times 9 = \boxed{}$.

Are you looking for a factor or a product?

Solution: _____

💬 **Pair/Share**

Explain how you solved this problem.

16 Mrs. Tobin needs 30 juice boxes for her class. The juice boxes come in packages of 6. How many packages does she need? Solve $30 \div 6 = \boxed{}$. Circle the letter of the correct answer.

A 4

B 5

C 6

D 36

Pia chose **D** as the correct answer. How did she get that answer?

_____

_____

_____

Do you know a multiplication fact that can help you solve this problem?

💬 **Pair/Share**

Does Pia's answer make sense?

Solve the problems.

1   Which does NOT belong to the same fact family as $12 \div \boxed{} = 4$?

   A $12 \div 3 = \boxed{}$

   B $\boxed{} \times 2 = 12$

   C $4 \times \boxed{} = 12$

   D $12 \div 4 = \boxed{}$

2   Which multiplication fact can you use to solve $5 = 20 \div \boxed{}$?

   A $5 \times 5 = 25$

   B $4 \times 5 = 20$

   C $5 + 15 = 20$

   D $6 \times 4 = 24$

3   Jan and Jon pick 18 apples. They share them equally. Which facts can be used to find the number of apples each person gets? Circle the letter for all that apply.

   A $6 \times 3 = 18$

   B $2 \times 9 = 18$

   C $18 \div 2 = 9$

   D $18 \div 3 = 6$

   E $18 \div 9 = 2$

©Curriculum Associates, LLC   Copying is not permitted.

4   For items 4a–4d, choose *Yes* or *No* to show whether putting the number 8 in the box would make the equation true.

    a. $9 \times \boxed{} = 64$ ☐ Yes   ☐ No

    b. $6 \times \boxed{} = 48$ ☐ Yes   ☐ No

    c. $56 \div \boxed{} = 8$ ☐ Yes   ☐ No

    d. $32 \div \boxed{} = 4$ ☐ Yes   ☐ No

5   Ho says that some fact families have only one multiplication equation and one division equation. Fill in the blanks to show an example.

    _____ $\times$ _____ $=$ _____   _____ $\div$ _____ $=$ _____

6   Sasha has 32 stickers to use in her scrapbook. The scrapbook has 8 pages, and she wants to put the same number of stickers on each page. Write two multiplication facts Sasha can use to find how many stickers to put on each page.

    Answer _____

    _____

✓ **Self Check**   *Go back and see what you can check off on the Self Check on page 1.*

©Curriculum Associates, LLC   Copying is not permitted.

Lesson 7 Part 1: Introduction

Understand Patterns

CCSS
3.OA.D.9

What are patterns?

A pattern is something that repeats. Sometimes we see patterns in shapes or letters. Other times numbers make a pattern. Patterns can also be found when we use numbers to add, subtract, multiply, or divide.

You can also see patterns in things around you. Look at the line of kids below.

🔍 **Think** How can you describe a pattern?

Telling about what repeats in a pattern is called the rule. The rule for the line of kids is boy, boy, girl.

You can also use numbers to describe this pattern.

> **What do you add to get to the next number in the pattern?** _____

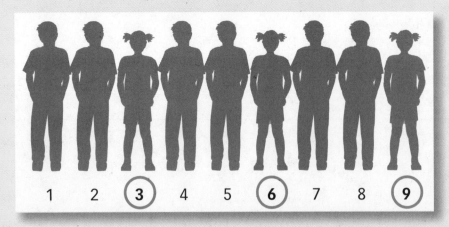

1   2   ③   4   5   ⑥   7   8   ⑨

The numbers 3, 6, 9, . . . tell where the girls are in line. Because the numbers in the pattern do not repeat, you need to look for something that is done over and over to get from one number to the next number.

©Curriculum Associates, LLC   Copying is not permitted.

🔍 **Think** How do you know what numbers come next in a pattern?

You can use the rule to figure out what other numbers are in the pattern. To get from one number to the next in the pattern, you add 3.

The pattern is continued in the chart below.

1	2	3	4	5	6	7	8	9	10
11	12	13	14	15	16	17	18	19	20
21	22	23	24	25	26				

Putting the numbers in a chart helps me notice things I might not see if I just made a list of numbers.

You may also notice other things about the pattern that can help you figure out what numbers come next.

The numbers form diagonals in the hundreds chart. You can use them to tell the next number in the pattern is 27.

The numbers in this pattern also alternate: even, odd, even, odd. Since 27 is odd, you know that the number that comes after 27 will be even.

✏️ **Reflect**

1 Write your own number pattern that has at least six numbers in it. Then, describe the rule and one other thing you notice about the pattern.

_____

_____

©Curriculum Associates, LLC   Copying is not permitted.

🔍 **Explore It**

Use the information below to help you think about patterns in addition.

> Rick has a pack of 100 baseball cards and likes to sort them into 2 piles.
> He notices that when he has a pile of 20 cards, the other pile has 80 cards.
> When he has a pile of 30 cards, the other pile has 70. When he has a pile
> of 40 cards, the other pile has 60. Finally, when he has a pile of 50 cards,
> the other pile has 50 too.

2 Rick shaded 20 squares in the first grid to show how many baseball cards were in the first set of piles he made. Shade the rest of the grids to show the other sets of piles.

 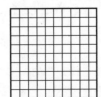 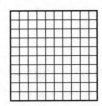

3 What do the shaded squares show in each grid?

_____

4 What do the white squares show in each grid?

_____

5 What happens to the number of shaded squares as you move from one grid to the next? _____

6 What happens to the number of white squares as you move from one grid to the next? _____

7 Describe the rule for this pattern.

_____

_____

©Curriculum Associates, LLC　Copying is not permitted.

Talk About It

Solve the problems below as a group.

8 The grid on the left shows Rick's piles of 30 and 70. The grid on the right shows Rick's piles of 40 and 60. Shade the grid in the middle to show what happens if Rick put 35 in one pile.

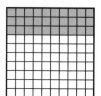   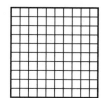

9 Explain how Rick can use the pattern to find the number of cards in the other pile.

_____

_____

_____

10 Describe what happens in addition patterns where the sum stays the same but you change the numbers you add together.

_____

_____

_____

Try It Another Way

Work with your group to use the tables to show patterns with addends and sums.

11 Fill in the missing numbers.

Addend	Addend	Sum
20	80	100
30		100
	65	100
	60	100
50		100

12 Fill in the missing numbers.

Addend	Addend	Sum
5	20	25
8		25
10		25
16		25
20		25

©Curriculum Associates, LLC   Copying is not permitted.

Connect It

13 **Explain:** Izzy noticed a pattern in the addition table. She found a diagonal that had all 5s in it. Fill in the table below on the right to show the addends.

+	0	1	2	3	4	5
0	0	1	2	3	4	5
1	1	2	3	4	5	6
2	2	3	4	5	6	7
3	3	4	5	6	7	8
4	4	5	6	7	8	9
5	5	6	7	8	9	10

Addend	Addend	Sum
0		5
	4	5
	3	5
	2	5
4		5
5		5

Explain why the 5s form a diagonal line.

_____

_____

_____

14 **Examine:** Jace counted to 50 by fives. Annabel counted to 50 by tens. What numbers did both Jace and Annabel say? _____

Explain why some of the numbers they said were the same.

_____

_____

15 **Determine:** Pat saw an odd number of birds on Monday and an even number of birds on Tuesday. Is the total number of birds he saw odd or even? _____

Explain how you know this, even though you don't know how many birds he saw.

_____

_____

_____

_____

©Curriculum Associates, LLC   Copying is not permitted.

Put It Together

16 Look at the multiplication table below.

	0	1	2	3	4	5	6	7	8	9
0	0	0	0	0	0	0	0	0	0	0
1	0	1	2	3	4	5	6	7	8	9
2	0	2	4	6	8					18
3	0		6	9	12	15	18	21	24	27
4	0	4		12		20		28		36
5	0	5		15		25		35		45
6	0	6	12	18	24		36		48	54
7	0	7	14	21	28	35		49		63
8	0				40	48		64		
9	0	9	18		36	45	54	63		81

A Fill in the missing numbers.

B Describe a pattern you see in the table.

_____

_____

_____

C Explain why the pattern works the way it does.

_____

_____

_____

©Curriculum Associates, LLC   Copying is not permitted.

Solve the problems.

1 Which number makes the number sentence true?

$$\boxed{} \div 2 = 10$$

A 5

B 8

C 12

D 20

2 Which number sentence can help Jack find $27 \div 9$?

A $9 - \boxed{} = 27$

B $9 \times \boxed{} = 27$

C $9 \div \boxed{} = 27$

D $9 + \boxed{} = 27$

3 Which number sentences are true? Circle the letter for all that apply.

A $6 \times 4 \times 2 = 6 \times 2 \times 4$

B $6 \times 4 \times 2 = 6 \times 8$

C $6 \times 8 = (6 \times 2) + (6 \times 4)$

D $6 \times 8 = (6 \times 4) + (6 \times 4)$

E $6 \times 8 = (2 \times 8) + (4 \times 8)$

4 Each classroom in a school has 6 rows of desks with 5 desks in each row. How many desks are in a classroom?

_____ desks

5 Leo had 48 ounces of juice. The juice was measured equally into cups. Each cup held 6 ounces of juice. How many cups of juice did Leo have?

_____ cups of juice

©Curriculum Associates, LLC   Copying is not permitted.

6

Part A

Juanita has 24 pencils. She packs boxes with 6 pencils in each box. Fill in the blanks to write a division sentence that shows the number of boxes she used.

_____ ÷ _____ = _____

Part B

Juanita has 24 more pencils. She wants to pack them into 8 boxes so that each box has the same number of pencils. Write and solve a division sentence that shows how many pencils Juanita will need to pack into each box.

Answer _____

7

Part A

Part of a multiplication table is shown below.

	1	2	3	4	5	6	7	8	9	10
5	5	10	15	20	25	30	35	40	45	50
6	6	12	18	24	30	36	42	48	54	60
7	7	14	21	28	35	42	49	56	63	70

What is the pattern of odd and even numbers in each row?

_____

_____

Part B

Why is the pattern of odd and even numbers in Row 6 different from the patterns in the other two rows?

_____

_____

©Curriculum Associates, LLC   Copying is not permitted.

Performance Task

Answer the questions and show all your work on separate paper.

Madelyn, William, Hannah, and Asher are trying to decide how to display erasers at the school store. Asher said that they came in 2 packages, and that each package had 24 erasers.

William says that they can lay them out in 4 rows with 12 erasers in each row. Hannah thinks that they should display them in 7 rows with 7 erasers in each row. Madelyn wants to lay them out in two groups: 3 rows with 6 erasers in each row on one table, and 5 rows with 6 erasers in each row on another table.

Tell whether each person's idea will work and explain why or why not.

☑ **CHECKLIST**

Did you . . .

☐ Write equations to represent the arrangements?

☐ Draw diagrams?

☐ Use complete sentences?

Reflect on Mathematical Practices

After you complete the task, choose one of the following questions to answer.

1. **Persevere** How did you decide what to do first to solve this problem?

2. **Model** What models helped you solve this problem?

©Curriculum Associates, LLC   Copying is not permitted.

Have you ever counted to 100 by tens while playing hide-and-seek? 10, 20, 30, 40, and so on. Add ten each time and you will reach 100 in no time! Could you count by tens if you start at 8? Sure, add 10 each time. 8, 18, 28, 38, 48, and so on. You might notice that the only thing that changes as you add 10 each time is the value of the tens digit.

In this unit, you will add and multiply numbers. You will find that understanding place value and knowing the value of each digit that makes up a number can be a big help when solving addition and multiplication problems.

✓ Self Check

Before starting this unit, check off the skills you know below. As you complete each lesson, see how many more you can check off!

I can:	Before this unit	After this unit
use place value to round numbers to the nearest 10 and to the nearest 100, for example: • 315 rounded to the nearest 10 is 320 • 826 rounded to the nearest 100 is 800.	☐	☐
use place value to add and subtract, for example: 29 + 48 = (20 + 40) + (9 + 8).	☐	☐
solve word problems by adding and subtracting using place value.	☐	☐
use place value to multiply, for example: $6 \times 40 = 6 \times (4 \times 10)$ $\qquad = (6 \times 4) \times 10$ $\qquad = 24 \times 10$ $\qquad = 240$	☐	☐

©Curriculum Associates, LLC   Copying is not permitted.

Lesson 8   Part 1: Introduction

Use Place Value to Round Numbers

You know that three-digit numbers are formed by groups of hundreds, tens, and ones. Take a look at this problem.

Look at the number 384. Between which two tens does it fall? Between which two hundreds does it fall? You can show 384 in a place-value chart.

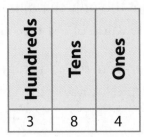

Hundreds	Tens	Ones
3	8	4

🔍 Explore It

Use math you already know to solve the problem.

- How many tens are in 384? _____

    What is the next greatest number of tens? _____

- How do you write both of these numbers of tens as numerals? _____

- Between which two tens does 384 fall? _____

- How many hundreds are in 384? _____
  What is the next greatest number of hundreds _____

- How do you write both of these numbers of hundreds as numerals? _____

- Between which two hundreds does 384 fall? _____

©Curriculum Associates, LLC   Copying is not permitted.

Find Out More

Rounding is finding a number that is close to another number. The reason for rounding is to find numbers that are easy to work with. That's why you round three-digit numbers to the nearest ten or hundred. A number line can help you understand how rounding is done.

Rounding to the Nearest Ten

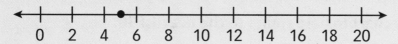

The number line shows that 8 is nearer to 10 than to 0. It also shows that 13 is nearer to 10 than to 20. What about 5? The dot is at 5. It is halfway between 0 and 10. The rule for rounding is that 5 rounds up to 10.

Rounding to the Nearest Hundred

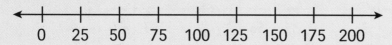

The number line can help you see that 25 is nearer to 0 than to 100. Also, 175 is nearer to 200 than to 100. Even though 50 is halfway between 0 and 100, the rules says that it rounds to 100. But, 49 is nearer to 0 than to 100.

Reflect

1 Use the number 145. What ten does it round to? What is the nearest hundred? Explain how you found your answer.

_____

_____

_____

©Curriculum Associates, LLC   Copying is not permitted.

Read the problem below. Then explore different ways to round to the nearest 10.

Ally keeps track of the time she spends doing homework. She rounds the times to the nearest ten minutes. If Ally spent 37 minutes on her homework, how would she record this time?

Picture It

You can use a hundreds chart to help round to the nearest 10.

37 is between the tens 30 and 40.

1	2	3	4	5	6	7	8	9	10
11	12	13	14	15	16	17	18	19	20
21	22	23	24	25	26	27	28	29	30
31	32	33	34	35	36	37	38	39	40
41	42	43	44	45	46	47	48	49	50
51	52	53	54	55	56	57	58	59	60
61	62	63	64	65	66	67	68	69	70
71	72	73	74	75	76	77	78	79	80
81	82	83	84	85	86	87	88	89	90
91	92	93	94	95	96	97	98	99	100

Solve It

Use what you know about rounding to solve the problem.

The halfway point between 30 and 40 is 35.

37 is greater than 35, so round 37 up to 40.

Ally would record the time as 40 minutes.

©Curriculum Associates, LLC   Copying is not permitted.

Connect It

Now you can round three-digit numbers to the nearest 10.

Round 943 to the nearest ten.

2 The number 943 is between what two tens? _____

3 What number is halfway between these two tens? _____

4 Is 943 less than or greater than the halfway number? _____

5 Will you round up or round down? _____

6 What is 943 rounded to the nearest ten? _____

7 Explain how to round a number to the nearest ten.

_____

_____

_____

_____

Try It

8 What is 106 rounded to the nearest ten? _____

9 Round to the nearest ten. What is a number less than 180 that rounds to 180?

_____

_____

What is a number greater than 180 that rounds to 180?

_____

_____

Read the problem below. Then explore different ways to round to the nearest 100.

> There are 236 third graders at Huron Elementary School. What is 236 rounded to the nearest hundred?

Picture It

Use place-value drawings to show the number you are rounding.

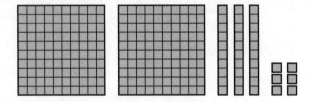

236 has 2 hundreds, so it is between 200 and 300.

The drawing shows that 236 is 2 hundreds + 3 tens + 6 ones.

Solve It

Use what you know about rounding to solve the problem.

There are 10 tens in each hundred. Halfway between 0 tens and 10 tens is 5 tens.

236 has 3 tens, and 3 tens is less than 5 tens. Round 236 down.

236 rounded to the nearest 100 is 200.

©Curriculum Associates, LLC   Copying is not permitted.

Connect It

Now you can round another three-digit number to the nearest 100.

Round 358 to the nearest hundred.

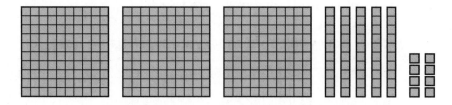

10 The number 358 is between what two hundreds? _____

11 How many tens are in 358? _____

12 What number of tens is halfway between hundreds? _____

13 What is 358 rounded to the nearest hundred? _____

14 Did you round up or round down? Explain how you knew which hundred to round to.

_____

_____

_____

Try It

15 What is 476 rounded to the nearest hundred? _____

16 You are rounding to the nearest 100. What numbers less than 100 would round to 100?

_____

Study the model below. Then solve problems 17–19.

The blocks show the number of hundreds, tens, and ones in 362.

💬**Pair/Share**

Explain why 362 was rounded up or down.

Student Model

Mr. Watson's shoe store has 362 pairs of shoes in stock. What is 362 rounded to the nearest ten?

Look at how you could show your work using base-ten blocks.

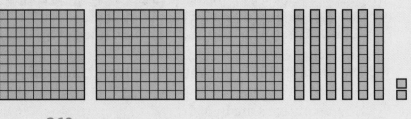

Solution: ___360___

Read the problem carefully. Are you rounding to the nearest 10 or 100?

💬**Pair/Share**

Which digit in the number helps you decide whether to round up or down?

17 The school cafeteria has 879 plates. What is this number rounded to the nearest hundred?

Show your work.

Solution: _____

©Curriculum Associates, LLC   Copying is not permitted.

18 Eddie picked out a TV for $479 and a DVD player for $129. He rounded each price to the nearest $10 to estimate the total cost. What is each price rounded to the nearest $10?

Show your work.

Solution: _____

Between what two tens is 479?

Pair/Share
Why would Eddie round the prices?

19 There are 416 third grade students at the Lincoln School. What is this number rounded to the nearest hundred?

A 400

B 410

C 420

D 500

Lien chose **C** as the correct answer. How did he get that answer?

_____

_____

_____

How many hundreds and tens are in the number?

Pair/Share
What kinds of mistakes could Lien have made?

Solve the problems.

1 Jolon scored 194 points during the basketball season. Round his points to the nearest hundred. Jolon scored almost how many points?

 A 100

 B 180

 C 190

 D 200

2 Round to the nearest 10. Which number will NOT round to 590?

 A 596

 B 594

 C 588

 D 585

3 Tell whether each sentence is *True* or *False*.

 a. 496 rounded to the nearest 100 is 500. ☐ True ☐ False

 b. 496 rounded to the nearest 10 is 500. ☐ True ☐ False

 c. 205 rounded to the nearest 10 is 300. ☐ True ☐ False

 d. 745 rounded to the nearest 100 is 800. ☐ True ☐ False

©Curriculum Associates, LLC Copying is not permitted.

4 Which of the following numbers will round to 250 when rounded to the nearest 10? Circle the letter for all that apply.

A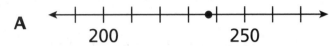

200   250

B

Hundreds	Tens	Ones
2	2	6

C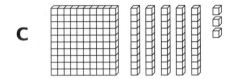

D   259

E   245

5 When rounding to the nearest hundred, what is the least whole number that rounds to 400? What is the greatest whole number that rounds to 400?

Answer _____

_____

6 A total of 778 tickets were sold to a charity event. A newspaper article rounded 778 when it listed the number of tickets sold. Round the number of tickets to the nearest 10 and to the nearest 100. Fill in the blanks to show about how many tickets were sold.

Rounded to the nearest 10, almost _____ tickets were sold.

Rounded to the nearest 100, almost _____ tickets were sold.

✓ **Self Check** *Go back and see what you can check off on the Self Check on page 61.*

©Curriculum Associates, LLC   Copying is not permitted.

Lesson 9   Part 1: Introduction

Use Place Value to Add and Subtract

CCSS
3.NBT.A.2

In this lesson you will add and subtract by breaking apart and adding numbers. Look at the problem below.

Rodney has 147 songs on his MP3 player, and Elaine has 212 songs on her MP3 player. How many songs do Rodney and Elaine have in all?

Rodney's songs: Elaine's songs:

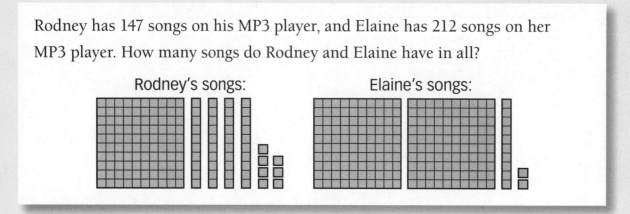

🔍 Explore It

Use the math you already know to solve the problem.

- 147 can be written as $100 + 40 + 7$. Write 212 in the same way. _____

- Add the hundreds from both numbers. _____

- Add the tens from both numbers. _____

- Add the ones from both numbers. _____

- Explain how to find the number of songs Rodney and Elaine have in all.

  _____

  _____

©Curriculum Associates, LLC   Copying is not permitted.

🔍 Find Out More

There are different ways to break apart numbers. You decide the way that works best for the problem you need to solve.

$147 = (100 + 40 + 7), (100 + 20 + 20 + 7), \text{ or } (140 + 7)$

$7 = (1 + 6), (2 + 5), \text{ or } (3 + 4)$

Breaking apart numbers can make it easier to add and subtract. You can add and subtract hundreds and hundreds, tens and tens, and ones and ones.

Here are two ways to show the sum of 147 and 212:

$147 \longrightarrow 100 + 40 + 7$
$212 \longrightarrow \underline{200 + 10 + 2}$
$ 300 + 50 + 9 \text{ or } 359$

$$
\begin{array}{r}
147 \\
+\ 212 \\
\hline
9 \\
50 \\
\underline{300} \\
359
\end{array}
$$

$9 \longrightarrow$ 7 ones + 2 ones = 9 ones
$50 \longrightarrow$ 4 tens + 1 ten = 5 tens
$300 \longrightarrow$ 1 hundred + 2 hundreds = 3 hundreds

✏️ Reflect

1 Show how to break apart numbers to add $240 + 130$.

_____

_____

_____

Read the addition problem below. Then explore different ways to find sums of three-digit numbers.

Garcia has 130 trading cards. Mark has 280 trading cards. How many trading cards do Garcia and Mark have in all?

Picture It

You can use base-ten blocks to help add three-digit numbers.

The model below shows the 130 trading cards Garcia has.

The model below shows the 280 trading cards Mark has.

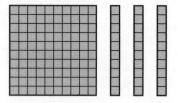
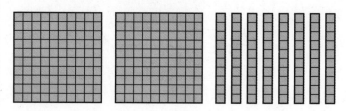

The model below shows the total number of trading cards Garcia and Mark have.

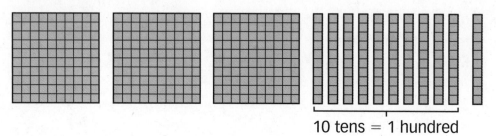

10 tens = 1 hundred

Regroup 11 tens as 1 hundred + 1 ten. Add 4 hundreds + 1 ten = 410.

Model It

You can also use place value to help add three-digit numbers.

```
   130
 + 280
```
   0 ⟶ There are 0 ones in both numbers.
 110 ⟶ 3 tens + 8 tens = 11 tens, or 1 hundred + 1 ten, or 110
 300 ⟶ 1 hundred + 2 hundreds = 3 hundreds, or 300
─────
 410

©Curriculum Associates, LLC   Copying is not permitted.

Connect It

Now you will solve the problem from the previous page by showing regrouping with digits.

2 Add the ones, 0 + 0. Record the sum in the ones place below the line.

3 Add the tens. How many tens are in the sum?

_____

How do you regroup the tens as hundreds and tens?

_____ hundred and _____ ten

	1	3	0
+	2	8	0

4 Record the regrouped tens in the addition problem. Put the number of hundreds in the box above the hundreds column. Write the number of tens below the line in the tens column.

5 Now add the hundreds. Be sure to include the hundred in the box. What numbers do you need to add?

_____

Record the sum in the hundreds column.

6 How could you use this method to add when both tens and ones need to be regrouped? Show with the problem 158 + 363.

	1	5	8
+	3	6	3

Try It

Use what you just learned about regrouping to solve these problems.

7

	1	9	2
+	1	1	4

8

	2	8	4
+	2	5	8

Read the subtraction problem below. Then explore different ways to find the difference of 3-digit numbers.

Julie kept track of the weather for 365 days. It was sunny for 186 of the days. How many days were not sunny?

Picture It

You can use base-ten blocks to help subtract three-digit numbers.

This model shows 365 − 186. All the blocks show 365. One ten and one hundred are regrouped. The blocks crossed out show 186.

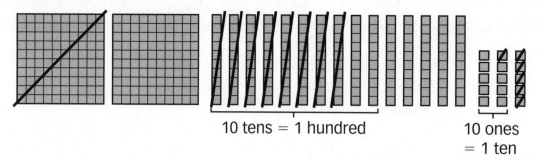

10 tens = 1 hundred

10 ones = 1 ten

Blocks that are left: 1 hundred + 7 tens + 9 ones = 179

Model It

You can also use place value to help subtract three-digit numbers.

Write each number as hundreds, tens, and ones.

365 = 3 hundreds + 6 tens + 5 ones, or
      2 hundreds + 16 tens + 5 ones, or
      2 hundreds + 15 tens + 15 ones

186 = **1 hundred + 8 tens + 6 ones**

Subtract hundreds, tens, and ones.

2 hundreds − 1 hundred = 1 hundred
15 tens − 8 tens = 7 tens
15 ones − 6 ones = 9 ones

Combine these differences.

1 hundred + 7 tens + 9 ones = 179

©Curriculum Associates, LLC   Copying is not permitted.

Connect It

Now you will solve the problem from the previous page by regrouping and subtracting hundreds, tens, and ones.

Step 1: $365 = 300 + 60 + 5$ Step 1: $186 = 100 + 80 + 6$

Step 2: $200 + 160 + 5$

Step 3: $200 + 150 + 15$

9 Look at 365. Are there enough hundreds, tens, and ones to subtract 186?

_____

10 Explain the regrouping used to go from Step 1 to Step 2.

_____

Explain the regrouping used to go from Step 2 to Step 3.

_____

11 Subtract each place: $200 - 100 =$ _____ $150 - 80 =$ _____ $15 - 6 =$ _____

Now find what is left by adding the three differences: _____

12 Explain how to subtract three-digit numbers when you need to regroup hundreds and tens.

_____

_____

Try It

Use what you just learned about subtraction to solve these problems. Show your work on a separate sheet of paper.

13   362
     $-\ 125$

14   425
     $-\ 289$

©Curriculum Associates, LLC   Copying is not permitted.

Read the subtraction problem below. Then explore how to subtract by adding on.

Perez has 205 flower seeds. He plants 137 seeds. How many flower seeds does Perez have left?

Model It

You can use a number line to subtract by adding on.

To solve the problem, subtract 205 − 137. You can also solve the problem with the addition equation 137 + ☐ = 205. Use a number line to add on to 137 to get to 205.

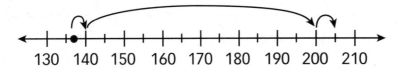

130 140 150 160 170 180 190 200 210

Find the numbers that you add to get to the next number.

137 + 3 = 140 ⟶ Add on a number to get to the next ten.

140 + 60 = 200 ⟶ Add on a number to get to the hundred you are looking for.

200 + 5 = 205 ⟶ Add on a number to get to the total.

You added 3 + 60 + 5 = 68.

137 + 68 = 205

©Curriculum Associates, LLC   Copying is not permitted.

💡 Connect It

Now you can use a chart to track the numbers you add on.

	Hundreds	Tens	Ones
137			3
140			
200			
205			

15 Start at 137. What is the next 10? _____ How many ones do you add to get to the next ten? _____

16 What do you add to get to the hundred you need? Write the answer in the chart.

17 Now what do you add to get to 205? Write your answer in the chart.

18 Write a number sentence to show what you added. _____

19 Explain how you would add on to subtract 202 − 195.

_____

_____

_____

✏️ Try It

Use what you just learned about using place value to solve these problems. Show your work on a separate sheet of paper.

20 Edith had $600. She spent $84. How much does Edith have left? _____

21 Juan sent and received 800 text messages. He sent 379 text messages. How many text messages did Juan receive? _____

©Curriculum Associates, LLC   Copying is not permitted.

Study the model below. Then solve problems 22–24.

Student Model

The student broke apart 617 and 219 into hundreds, tens, and ones. That makes it easy to add the two numbers.

On Monday, a flower store sold 617 roses. On Tuesday, 279 roses were sold. How many roses were sold on Monday and Tuesday?

Look at how you could show your work by breaking apart 617 and 279.

$$617 + 279 = (600 + 200) + (10 + 70) + (7 + 9)$$
$$= 800 + 80 + 16$$
$$= 896$$

Solution: __896 roses__

Pair/Share
How else could you solve this problem?

How many magnets does Roger have?

22 Diana has 109 magnets. Roger has 56 more magnets than Diana. How many magnets do Diana and Roger have in all?

Show your work.

Pair/Share
How did you decide which operation to use?

Solution: _____

©Curriculum Associates, LLC   Copying is not permitted.

23 Corey works 144 hours a month. He has worked 72 hours so far this month. How many more hours does Corey have to work this month?

Show your work.

Do you need to regroup?

Solution: _____

💬**Pair/Share**

How can you use adding on to solve this problem?

24 Chad practiced batting for 205 minutes this week. Doug practiced batting for 110 minutes. How many more minutes did Chad practice than Doug?

A 90 minutes

B 95 minutes

C 195 minutes

D 315 minutes

Sam chose **D** as the correct answer. How did he get that answer?

_____

_____

_____

_____

To find how many more minutes, should you add or subtract?

💬**Pair/Share**

How can you use estimation to see if Sam's answer makes sense?

Solve the problems.

1 Mr. Coleman drove 129 miles on Monday. He drove 78 more miles on Tuesday than on Monday. How many miles did Mr. Coleman drive altogether on Monday and Tuesday?

A   51

B   207

C   285

D   336

2 Which of the following diagrams or solutions represent the difference 354 − 298? Circle the letter for all that apply.

A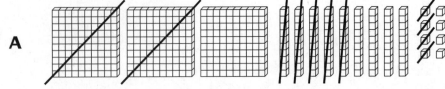

B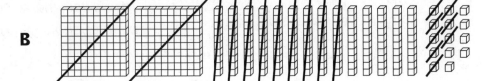

C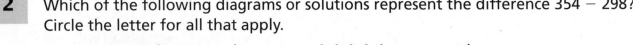

D   2 hundreds − 2 hundreds = 0 hundreds
15 tens − 9 tens = 6 tens
14 ones − 8 ones = 6 ones

E   3 hundreds − 2 hundreds = 1 hundred
15 tens − 9 tens = 6 tens
14 ones − 8 ones = 6 ones

©Curriculum Associates, LLC   Copying is not permitted.

3   The number sentence below can be solved using tens and ones.

68 + 16 = _____?_____ tens and _____?_____ ones.

Select one number from each column to make the number sentence true.

Tens	Ones
○ 2	○ 4
○ 7	○ 9
○ 8	○ 12
○ 9	○ 14

4   Sam has 308 craft sticks. She buys a package of 625 craft sticks. She uses 245 craft sticks for a project. How many craft sticks does Sam have left?

Show your work.

Answer   Sam has _____ craft sticks left.

5   The digits in a three-digit number represent the amounts of hundreds, tens, and ones. Fill in the chart to show the amounts of hundreds, tens, and ones in the number 746.

Number	Hundreds	Tens	Ones
746			

Write a number that meets the following conditions.

• The number must be between 1 and 9.
• When the number is added to 746, the digit in the ones place of the sum is **less** than the ones place of 746.

_____

✓ **Self Check**   *Go back and see what you can check off on the Self Check on page 61.*

Lesson 10   Part 1: Introduction

Use Place Value to Multiply

In Lesson 6, you learned basic multiplication facts. In this lesson, you will learn how to multiply one-digit numbers by multiples of 10. Take a look at this problem.

There are 4 stacks of books on a table. Each stack has 20 books. How many books are there in all?

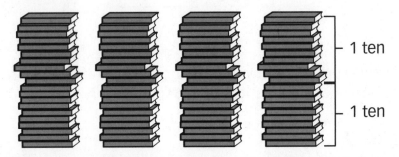

1 ten

1 ten

Explore It

Use the math you already know to solve the problem.

- How many books are in each stack? _____

- How many tens are in 20? _____

- How many groups of 2 tens are there in all the stacks? _____

- How can you find how many tens there are in all? _____

- How many tens are there? _____

- Explain how you can use skip counting to find the total number of books.

  _____

  _____

  _____

©Curriculum Associates, LLC   Copying is not permitted.

Find Out More

Multiplication is used to find the total when there are multiple groups with the same number in each group. You have learned some basic multiplication facts. These basic facts can help you multiply by tens.

The 4 stacks of 20 books can be shown using base-ten models and a multiplication expression.

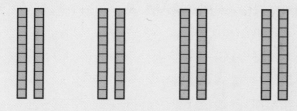

4 × 20

You can skip count to find the total number in several equal groups.

Skip count by 10 eight times.
10, 20, 30, 40, 50, 60, 70, 80

Skip count by 20 four times.
20, 40, 60, 80

You can also count on by groups of tens to multiply.

Count on by groups of 2 tens to find 4 × 20: 2 tens, 4 tens, 6 tens, 8 tens

8 tens is 80.

These strategies work well when the numbers are not too large. What if you were looking for the product of 8 × 80? Skip counting and counting on would take time and might be hard to track. This lesson will show you some quicker ways to multiply by tens.

Reflect

1 Explain how you could find the product of 3 × 50.

_____

_____

_____

©Curriculum Associates, LLC   Copying is not permitted.

Read the problem below. Then explore different ways to multiply by tens.

A sports store orders 4 boxes of baseball caps. Each box has 40 caps. How many baseball caps are in all 4 boxes?

🔍 Picture It

You can use base-ten blocks to help understand the problem.

4 boxes of baseball caps

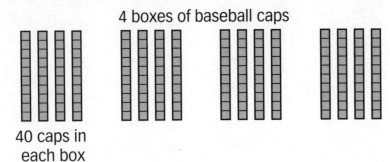

40 caps in each box

4 groups of 4 tens is 4 × 4 tens, or 16 tens.

16 tens is 160.

🔍 Model It

You can also use factors and grouping to multiply by tens.

Start with the factors from the problem: 4 × 40

40 can be broken down to the factors 4 × 10:   4 × (4 × 10)

You can change the grouping when you multiply: (4 × 4) × 10

Multiply 4 × 4:   16 × 10

                                            16 tens is 160.

©Curriculum Associates, LLC   Copying is not permitted.

Connect It

Now you will solve the problem from the previous page by breaking apart a two-digit number.

Below are 3 equal multiplication expressions from the previous page.

$$4 \times 40 \qquad 4 \times 4 \times 10 \qquad 16 \times 10$$

2 You can break apart 16 into 10 plus another number. Write the number in the blank: $\qquad 16 \times 10 = (10 + \underline{\hspace{1cm}}) \times 10$

3 You can multiply both numbers in the parentheses by 10. Write these numbers in the blanks: $\qquad = (\underline{\hspace{1cm}} \times 10) + (\underline{\hspace{1cm}} \times 10)$

4 Write the products in the blanks: $\qquad = \underline{\hspace{1cm}} + \underline{\hspace{1cm}}$

5 Add the products and write the sum in the blank: $\qquad = \underline{\hspace{1cm}}$

6 Below are some multiplication problems that you know or that you solved in this lesson.

$$4 \times 2 = 8 \qquad\qquad 4 \times 4 = 16 \qquad\qquad 16 \times 10 = 160$$

$$4 \times 2 \times 10 = 80 \qquad\qquad 4 \times 4 \times 10 = 160$$

Explain what happens to a number when you multiply it by 10.

_____

_____

Try It

Use what you just learned to solve these problems. Show your work on a separate sheet of paper.

7 $60 \times 8 = $ _____

8 $30 \times 7 = $ _____

Study the model below. Then solve problems 9–11.

Student Model

9 × 30 is:
9 groups of 3 tens, or
27 tens, or 270.

Robin planted 9 rows of flowers. Each row had 30 flowers. How many flowers did Robin plant in all?

Look at how you could show your work by changing the grouping when you multiply.

$$9 \times 30 = 9 \times (3 \times 10)$$
$$= (9 \times 3) \times 10$$
$$= 27 \times 10$$
$$= 270$$

Solution: **270 flowers**

Pair/Share

How could you use skip counting to solve this problem? Which way makes more sense?

How many groups of 5 tens are there?

9 Manu drives 50 miles each day to get to work and back home. How many miles does he drive in 5 days?

Show your work.

Pair/Share

How did you and your partner choose the way to solve this problem?

Solution: _____

©Curriculum Associates, LLC   Copying is not permitted.

10 Tanner shoots 90 free throws 6 times a week. How many free throws does she shoot each week?

Show your work.

How can you break apart 90 to multiply by 10?

Solution: _____

Pair/Share

How can you check that your answer is correct?

11 Raymond can type 40 words each minute. How many words can he type in 8 minutes?

A 32 words

B 48 words

C 320 words

D 360 words

Gina chose **B** as the correct answer. How did she get that answer?

_____

_____

_____

What basic multiplication fact can you use to solve the problem?

Pair/Share

How can the ones place help you decide if an answer makes sense?

Solve the problems.

1 Jerome averaged 30 yards per catch in his last football game. He caught 6 passes. How many yards did Jerome have?

A 5

B 18

C 180

D 200

2 There are 60 toothpicks in a jar. There are 3 jars in 1 box. How many toothpicks are in 2 boxes?

A 120

B 180

C 360

D 480

3 Choose **all** the expressions that are equal to 240.

A 40 × 6

B 4 × 60

C 30 × 8

D 80 × 3

E 2 × 40

©Curriculum Associates, LLC   Copying is not permitted.

4 A notebook has 80 sheets of paper. How many sheets of paper do 7 notebooks have?

_____ sheets of paper

5 At a pet store, there are 20 fish in each tank. How many fish are in 8 tanks?

Show your work.

Answer There are _____ fish in 8 tanks.

6 There are 40 nickels in each roll. Tao has 7 rolls of nickels. How many nickels does she have in all?

Show your work.

Answer Tao has _____ nickels.

✓ **Self Check** *Go back and see what you can check off on the Self Check on page 61.*

Solve the problems.

1 A school play ran for three nights. The total attendance at the play for the three nights was 388. What is this number rounded to the nearest ten?

A   300

B   380

C   390

D   400

2 At a high school football game, the visiting team had 274 fans. The home team had 173 more fans than the visiting team. How many fans did the home team have?

A   101

B   173

C   347

D   447

3 Solve the problem.

$703 - 285 = $ _____

4 Which statements are true? Circle the letter for all that apply.

A   645 rounds to 600 when rounded to the nearest 10

B $289 + 543 = 832$

C $680 - 395 = 315$

D $4 \times 50 = 200$

©Curriculum Associates, LLC   Copying is not permitted.

5

Part A

What is 278 rounded to the nearest ten?

Answer _____

Part B

Draw a number line from 270 to 280 to show why your answer is correct.

Explain how the number line shows that your answer is correct.

_____

_____

6

Part A

A school has 7 buses. Each bus has 40 seats. Fill in the missing numbers to find the total number of seats on the 7 buses.

$7 \times 40 = 7$ groups of _____ tens

7 groups of _____ tens = _____ tens

_____ tens = _____ seats on the school bus

Part B

Another school has 9 buses. Each bus has 50 seats. How many total seats are there on the 9 buses?

Answer _____ seats

©Curriculum Associates, LLC   Copying is not permitted.

Performance Task

Answer the questions and show all your work on separate paper.

Mr. Gemelli runs the school cafeteria. He needs your help ordering compostable lunch trays and bananas for the students' lunches. Here are Mr. Gemelli's instructions:

"I need 1 tray and 1 banana for each lunch ordered. I usually round the number of lunches for each day to the nearest 10 when I order bananas. I think this will give me some extra bananas in case students want more than one. I round each day's number to the nearest 100 when I order lunch trays because they are sold in packages of 100."

The table below shows the number of lunches ordered for each day this week.

	Monday	Tuesday	Wednesday	Thursday	Friday
# of lunches	159	245	113	104	162

Use Mr. Gemelli's guidelines to make an order for trays and bananas. Write a letter to Mr. Gemelli telling him how many of each item he should order and explain how you know.

Reflect on Mathematical Practices

After you complete the task, choose one of the following questions to answer.

1. **Be Precise** How did you decide how to round the numbers in Mr. Gemelli's chart?

2. **Reason Mathematically** What strategies did you use to add the numbers in this problem?

©Curriculum Associates, LLC   Copying is not permitted.

People solve math problems every day. Most problems don't start out looking like 100 ÷ __?__ = 25 or 4 × 42 = __?__. It is more likely that a chef might have 5 cups of flour to make 3 cakes that each need 2 cups of flour. Does he have enough flour? Or a carpenter might need 80 inches of wood to finish a wall. She can buy wood in 16-inch pieces. How many pieces will she need to buy?

In this unit, you will solve problems in many different ways. You might write a math sentence or you might draw a picture. You might even be able to solve a problem by talking about it out loud until you find a solution.

✓ Self Check

Before starting this unit, check off the skills you know below. As you complete each lesson, see how many more you can check off!

I can:	Before this unit	After this unit
solve one-step word problems using multiplication or division.	☐	☐
model two-step word problems using the four operations.	☐	☐
solve two-step word problems using the four operations.	☐	☐

©Curriculum Associates, LLC   Copying is not permitted.

Lesson 11   Part 1: Introduction 👥

Solve One-Step Word Problems Using Multiplication and Division

You have learned about different ways to show multiplication and division. In this lesson, you will learn how to solve multiplication and division word problems. Take a look at this problem.

Write a word problem about the picture below.

🔍 Explore It

Use the math you already know to solve the problem.

- Think of the picture as equal groups. What does it show? _____
  _____

- Now think of the picture as an array. What does it show? _____
  _____

- Write the fact family that the picture shows. Make sure you use 2 multiplication equations and 2 division equations.
  _____

- Why can the picture be used to describe both multiplication and division?
  _____
  _____

- Pick one of the multiplication or division equations you wrote in the fact family. Use this equation to write a word problem about the picture. _____
  _____
  _____

©Curriculum Associates, LLC   Copying is not permitted.

Find Out More

Sometimes you can write a multiplication sentence to help you solve a word problem. Other times you can write a multiplication or division sentence. Look at these examples:

Example 1:

There are 6 bananas on each bunch. How many bananas are in 2 bunches?

You can solve this problem using $2 \times 6 = ?$ or $6 \times 2 = ?$

Example 2:

2 bunches have a total of 12 bananas. Each bunch has the same number of bananas. How many bananas are on each bunch?

You can solve this problem using $2 \times ? = 12$ or $12 \div 2 = ?$

Example 3:

Each bunch has 6 bananas. If there are 12 bananas, how many bunches are there?

You can solve this problem using $6 \times ? = 12$ or $12 \div 6 = ?$

Reflect

1 Write a multiplication sentence and a division sentence that could help you solve the problem below. Then solve the problem.

A hat rack has 2 rows of hooks. Each row has the same number of hooks. The rack has 10 hooks in all. How many hooks are in each row?

_____

Read the problem below. Then explore different ways to solve problems about equal groups.

There are 24 students in class. The students form 4 groups to play in a math game. Each group has an equal number of students. How many students are in each group?

 **Picture It**

You can use a drawing to show and solve problems about equal groups.

Make 4 groups of 1 person each. Add 1 person at a time to each group until there are 24 people.

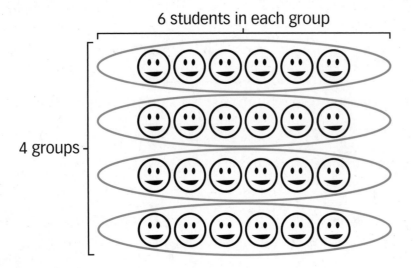

6 students in each group

4 groups

Model It

You can also use words to show and solve problems about equal groups.

Make notes about the problem:

   4 groups or teams

   _____ in each group or team

   24 students in all.

Use multiplication or division to find the number in each group:

   $4 \times 6 = 24$ or $24 \div 4 = 6$

©Curriculum Associates, LLC   Copying is not permitted.

Connect It

Now you will solve the problem from the previous page.

2 What does 24 in the problem stand for? _____

What does 4 stand for? _____

3 What is the unknown in the problem? _____

4 Use a letter to stand for the unknown. Write a division equation that can be used to solve the problem. _____ Write a related multiplication problem. _____

5 What is the solution? Explain how you found your answer.

_____

6 What if the problem is changed to the one below?

> There are 24 students, and the gym teacher wants to make groups of 6 students each. How many groups will there be?

Explain how you can write a multiplication or division equation and solve this problem.

_____

_____

_____

Try It

Use what you just learned about using letters for unknowns to solve these problems. Show your work on a separate piece of paper.

7 Jenna has 30 photos of her friends. She puts 6 photos on each page in her album How many pages does Jenna use? _____

_____

8 There are 9 drawing kits on a table in the art room. Each kit has 4 stencils. How many stencils are there in all? _____

Read the problem below. Then explore different ways to solve problems about arrays.

A clothing store uses stacking crates for storing jeans. The manager orders 42 crates. Six crates will fit in one row along the wall. How many rows of crates will there be?

Picture It

You can use a drawing to show and solve problems about arrays.

Use an array. Show a row of 6. Add rows of 6 until you get to 42.

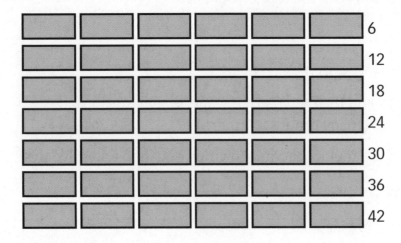

7 rows × 6 crates in a row = 42 crates

Model It

You can also use words to show and solve problems about arrays.

Make notes about the problem:

_____ rows

6 crates in each row

42 crates in all

Use multiplication or division to find the number of rows:

6 × 7 = 42 or 42 ÷ 6 = 7

©Curriculum Associates, LLC   Copying is not permitted.

🔍 Connect It

Now you will solve the problem from the previous page.

9 What do the numbers in the problem stand for? _____

_____

10 What is the unknown in the problem? _____

11 Use a letter to stand for the unknown. Write a division equation that can be used
to solve the problem. _____

Write a related multiplication problem. _____

12 Show and explain how to solve the problem. _____

_____

_____

13 Explain how you can use an array to solve this problem.

    There are 24 crayons in a box. There are 8 crayons in each row. How many rows
of crayons are there?

_____

_____

_____

✏️ Try It

**Use what you just learned about solving problems about arrays to solve these
problems. Show your work on a separate piece of paper.**

14 Grace's garden has 4 rows of tomatoes with 8 plants in each row. How many
tomato plants are in Grace's garden? _____

15 There are 20 students in gym class. The teacher lines up the students in 4 equal
rows for warm-up. How many students are in each row?

_____

©Curriculum Associates, LLC   Copying is not permitted.

Read the problem below. Then explore different ways to solve multiplication and division problems about tiling.

For an art project, Sean pasted colored squares side-by-side with no gaps. He used 48 squares and made 6 rows. Sean used the same number of squares in each row. How many squares did he put in each row?

Picture It

You can use a drawing to show and solve problems about tiling.

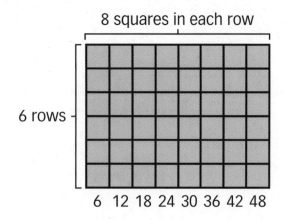

8 squares in each row

6 rows

6　12　18　24　30　36　42　48

48 squares ÷ 6 rows = 8 squares in a row

6 rows × 8 squares in a row = 48 squares

Model It

You can also use words to show and solve problems about tiling.

Make notes about the problem:

　6 rows

　_____ squares in each row

　48 squares

Use multiplication or division to find the number of squares in each row:

　$6 \times 8 = 48$ or $48 \div 6 = 8$

©Curriculum Associates, LLC　Copying is not permitted.

Connect It

Now you will solve the problem from the previous page.

16 What is the unknown in this problem? _____

17 Write a division equation with an unknown for this problem. _____

Write a related multiplication problem. _____

18 Show and explain how to solve the problem. _____

_____

19 In Part 3, you used the multiplication fact $6 \times 7 = 42$. How could you use this fact to find the solution to this problem?

_____

_____

_____

20 Sean changed his mind and decided to use 56 squares. He put them in 7 equal rows. Explain how you could use multiplication and division to find the number of squares in each row.

_____

_____

Try It

Use what you just learned about solving problems about tiling to solve these problems. Show your work on a separate piece of graph paper.

21 A walkway is made of square patio blocks. There are 2 rows of blocks with 9 blocks in each row. How many blocks are there in all?

_____

22 The blocks in problem 21 measure 1 foot on each side. How long is each row of blocks? How wide is the walkway?

_____

©Curriculum Associates, LLC   Copying is not permitted.

Study the model below. Then solve problems 23–25.

This problem can be solved using 3 × ? = 18 or 18 ÷ 3 = ?

Student Model

Troy has 18 homework problems to do. He has 3 days to finish the homework. If he does the same amount each day, how many problems will he do in a day?

Look at how you could show your work using a drawing.

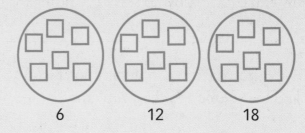

6   12   18

Solution: ___6 problems each day___

💬**Pair/Share**

Which equation did you use and why?

What does 28 stand for in the problem?

23 Mr. Rivera is posting students' papers on the bulletin board. There are 28 papers, and the bulletin board will hold 4 rows of papers. How many papers should Mr. Rivera put in each row?

Show your work.

💬**Pair/Share**

Did you multiply or divide to solve the problem?

Solution: _____

©Curriculum Associates, LLC   Copying is not permitted.

24 There are 54 players at a baseball clinic. The coach puts them into teams of 9 players. How many teams are there?

Show your work.

What fact do you know that includes both numbers in the problem?

Solution: _____

🗨 **Pair/Share**

How can you check that your answer is correct?

25 Mai eats 3 servings of fruit each day. How many servings of fruit does she eat in a week? Circle the letter of the correct answer. [Hint: 1 week = 7 days]

A   10 servings

B   18 servings

C   21 servings

D   24 servings

Harry chose **A** as the correct answer. How did he get that answer?

_____

_____

Should you multiply or divide to solve the problem?

🗨 **Pair/Share**

How did you figure out how Harry got his answer?

Solve the problems.

1   There are 8 socks in the dryer. How many pairs of socks is this?

  A   2

  B   4

  C   8

  D   16

2   Dana forms a rectangle with 15 square sticky notes. She puts 5 notes in each row. How many rows does she make?

  A   3

  B   5

  C   6

  D   10

3   Jane has 42 balloons. She is giving an equal number of balloons to 6 children.

  For 3a–3d, choose *Yes* or *No* to indicate whether each number sentence could be used to find the number of balloons Jane gives each child.

  a. $42 \times 6 = \square$ $\square$ Yes $\square$ No

  b. $6 \times \square = 42$ $\square$ Yes $\square$ No

  c. $6 \div \square = 42$ $\square$ Yes $\square$ No

  d. $42 \div 6 = \square$ $\square$ Yes $\square$ No

©Curriculum Associates, LLC   Copying is not permitted.

4   Choose **all** the situations that can be solved using 12 ÷ 4 = ☐.

   A   Brandon has 12 cookies. He gives the same number of cookies to each of his 4 friends. How many cookies does each friend get?

   B   Zoe has 12 folders. She wants to put 4 papers in each folder. How many papers does she need?

   C   Michael rides his bike 4 miles a day. How many days will it take him to ride 12 miles?

   D   Lilah has 12 tomatoes. She uses 4 tomatoes to make a salad. How many salads can she make?

5   Catrina used 25 green tiles to form a square in the middle of her kitchen floor. How many rows did she make? How many tiles did she put in each row?

Show your work.

Answer   Catrina made _____ rows with _____ tiles in each row.

6   There are 24 different stations to set up for field day. The principal wants the stations set up in equal rows. Should she use 3 rows or 5 rows? Explain.

_____

_____

_____

Show your work.

Answer   The principal should use _____ rows.

✓ **Self Check**   *Go back and see what you can check off on the Self Check on page 95.*

Lesson 12 Part 1: Introduction

Model Two-Step Word Problems Using the Four Operations

In this lesson, you will learn how to model two-step word problems that use all four operations. Take a look at this problem.

> Mr. Orr checks the pantry to see what he needs to get at the grocery store. There are 4 full boxes with 8 granola bars in each box. There are also 3 loose bars. How many granola bars are there in all?

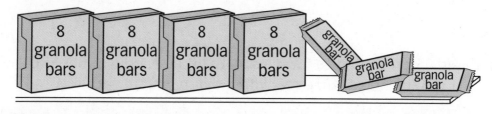

🔍 Explore It

Use the math you already know to solve the problem.

- How many boxes are on the shelf? _____

- How many granola bars are in each box? _____

- What operation do you use to find how many granola bars there are in all the boxes? Show how to find the total in all boxes.

  _____

- How many loose granola bars are on the shelf? _____

- What operation do you use to combine the boxed and loose granola bars? Show how to find the total.

  _____

©Curriculum Associates, LLC   Copying is not permitted.

🔍 Find Out More

When you solve two-step problems, you will need to use two operations. You might use multiplication and subtraction. You might use addition and division. You might even use addition and addition again!

Before you model the problem, you need to make sense of it. Think about the meaning of the answer. Think about what operation fits with each part of the problem. Let's look at the problem on the previous page.

There are 4 full boxes with 8 bars in each box. This sounds like an equal groups problem. It probably means that you will have to multiply or divide.

There are also 3 loose bars. There are equal groups and some extras. You will probably have to add or subtract the extras.

You can use different models to solve two-step problems. You can even use two different models for the two parts of the problem. Here are some ways to model the problem from the previous page.

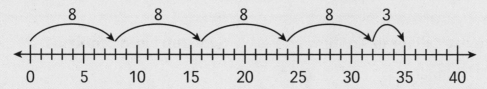

4 groups of 8: $4 \times 8 = 32$

3 more: $32 + 3 = 35$

✎ Reflect

1 Tell what operations you would use to solve this problem.

Zan has 5 packages, each with 6 balloons. She opens one package and gives 3 balloons to her brother. How many balloons does Zan have left?

_____

_____

Read the problem below. Then explore different ways to model two-step word problems when one operation is multiplication.

> Anya bought 5 baskets of apples. Each basket had 8 apples. She used 20 apples to make applesauce. How many apples are left?

Picture It

You can use a drawing to show and solve two-step word problems.

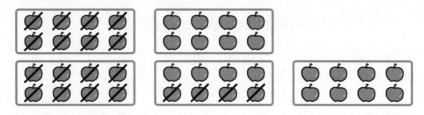

There are 2 groups of 8 and 1 group of 4 left: 2 × 8 + 4 = 20

Model It

You can also use a diagram to show and solve two-step word problems.

5 groups of 8 is a total of 40.

40				
8	8	8	8	8

Anya used 20 apples and left the rest.

40				
8	8	8	8	8
20			?	

40 − 20 = 20.

©Curriculum Associates, LLC   Copying is not permitted.

Connect It

Now you will model and solve the problem from the previous page by writing equations with unknowns.

2 How can you find the total number of apples Anya bought?

_____

Let *A* be the total number of apples that Anya bought. Write an equation that shows how to find *A*. _____

3 Let *L* be the number of apples that are left after Anya makes applesauce. If you start with *A*, how would you find *L*? What operation do you use?

_____

_____

4 How can you find the value of *A*? What is *A*? _____

5 Now, write and solve an equation to find the value of *L*. _____

6 Explain how you can use equations to model and solve two-step word problems.

_____

_____

_____

Try It

Use what you just learned about modeling problems using equations to model and solve these problems. Show your work on a separate piece of paper.

7 Josh had 4 five-dollar bills. His grandfather gave him a ten-dollar bill for his birthday. How much money does Josh have now?

_____

8 Vegetable plants are sold in packs of 4. A container holds 2 packs of plants. There are 8 containers on one shelf. How many total plants are on the shelf?

_____

Read the problem below. Then explore different ways to model two-step word problems when one operation is division.

Sam has a box with 12 cans of paint. There are 3 cans of paint on the shelf. He puts all of the cans of paint on the shelf in rows of 5. How many rows of paint cans does Sam make?

Picture It

You can use a drawing to show two-step word problems.

3 cans already on shelf

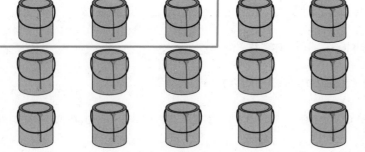

12 cans from box

15 cans of paint in rows of 5

3 rows

Model It

You can also use words and numbers to model two-step problems.

```
    12 cans in a box
 +   3 cans on a shelf
 ─────────────────────
    15 cans in all
```

15 cans ÷ 5 cans in each row = 3 rows

©Curriculum Associates, LLC   Copying is not permitted.

Connect It

Now you will model and solve the problem from the previous page by writing equations with unknowns.

9 How do you find the total number of cans of paint that Sam has?

_____

Let C be the total number of cans. Write an equation to find C. _____

10 How does Sam arrange the paint cans? _____

11 How can you find the number of rows? _____

Let R equal the number of rows. Write an equation to find R that includes C and R.

_____

12 How can you find the value of C? What is C? _____

Substitute the value of C into the equation you wrote in number 11. Solve the equation for R. _____

13 Explain how you can check that your answer is correct. Can you think of a way that uses multiplication? _____

_____

Try It

Use what you just learned about modeling problems using equations to model and solve these problems. Show your work on a separate piece of paper.

14 Rhea does a card trick. She puts 16 cards into 4 equal groups. Then she gives one group of cards to her friend. How many cards does Rhea have left?

_____

15 There are 16 water bottles that are divided equally between 2 teams. Each team has 4 players. Each player gets an equal number of water bottles. How many water bottles does each player get? _____

_____

Study the model below. Then solve problems 16–18.

Student Model

The bar model shows 3 packages of 8. The oval stands for the 3 cups of yogurt that were eaten.

Mrs. Alvarez buys 3 packages of yogurt, and each package includes 8 cups. On the way home from the store, her children eat 3 cups of yogurt. How many cups are left?

Look at how you could show your work using a diagram.

3 packages of 8 cups = 24 cups

24
8	8	8

Subtract 3 cups.

24
8	8	8
3	?

24 − 3 = 21

Solution: _There are 21 cups of yogurt left._

💬 Pair/Share

What equations could you write to solve this problem?

How can you find the total number of beads in both packages?

16 Jade has an unopened package of 24 beads. She also has 8 beads in a package that is already open. Jade puts all the beads together and divides them into 4 equal groups to share with her friends. How many beads are in each group?

Show your work.

💬 Pair/Share

How did you know what operations to use?

Solution: _____

©Curriculum Associates, LLC   Copying is not permitted.

17 There are 22 students in Mr. Flynn's class. Today, 2 students are absent. Mr Flynn puts the students that are there into 4 equal groups. How many students are in each group?

Show your work.

What do you do with the number of students who are absent?

Solution: _____

🗨**Pair/Share**

How can you check that your answer is correct?

18 Carmen and Abe act out a math problem. Carmen puts 7 counters each in 3 different cups. Abe takes away 3 counters. How many counters does Carmen have left? Circle the letter of the correct answer.

A 24

B 21

C 18

D 15

Jim chose **A** as the correct answer. How did he get that answer?

_____

_____

Should you multiply or divide to solve the problem?

🗨**Pair/Share**

How did you figure out how Harry got his answer?

Solve the problems.

1 Mr. Adkins has 2 packages, each with 6 batteries. He uses 4 of the batteries in a flashlight. How many batteries are left?

    A 16

    B 12

    C 10

    D 8

2 Ella, James, and Ray's grandmother gave them 24 dollars to divide equally. They spent the money during a 4-day vacation. They spent the same amount of money each day. How much did each person spend each day?

    A $1

    B $2

    C $4

    D $8

3 Amir is in charge of getting oranges for today's soccer game. He buys 2 bags with 6 oranges in each bag. He also buys 4 loose oranges.

Choose **all** the expressions that can be used to find the number of oranges Amir gets in all.

    A $2 \times 6 \times 4$

    B $2 + 6 + 4$

    C $6 + 6 + 4$

    D $2 \times 6 + 4$

    E $4 + 2 \times 6$

©Curriculum Associates, LLC   Copying is not permitted.

4 Marisa is keeping track of how many miles she runs. After her run on July 12, she had run a total of 7 miles. If she runs 3 miles each day after that, what is the total number of miles she will have run after her run on July 18?

_____ miles

5 There are 8 hooks in a display of pens. Each hook can hold 3 packages of pens and there are 3 pens in each package. If the display is completely full, how many pens does it hold?

Show your work.

Answer The display holds _____ pens.

6 Simone is stocking a shelf with salad dressing. She has one box with 30 bottles and another box with 18 bottles. She can fit 6 bottles in a row on the shelf. How many rows does she make using all the bottles in both boxes?

Show your work.

Answer Simone makes _____ rows of bottles.

 **Self Check** *Go back and see what you can check off on the Self Check on page 95.*

Lesson 13 Part 1: Introduction

CCSS
3.OA.D.8

Solve Two-Step Word Problems Using the Four Operations

In this lesson, you will apply what you know to two-step word problems with greater numbers. Take a look at this problem.

The Shirt Shack has 438 T-shirts right now. The owner orders 8 shirts each in 4 different sizes for the store. How many T-shirts will the store have when this order comes in? Write an equation that can be used to solve this problem.

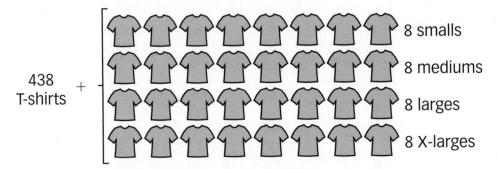

438 T-shirts +

8 smalls
8 mediums
8 larges
8 X-larges

🔍 Explore It

Use the math you already know to solve the problem.

_____ + (_____ × _____) = T

- How many T-shirts does the store have? _____ Write this number in the first blank.

- The first symbol is a +. What will you be adding? _____

- How many different sizes are in the owner's order? _____ Write this number in the second blank inside the parentheses.

- How many of each size shirt are in the owner's order? _____ Write this number in the first blank inside the parentheses.

- Why is there a multiplication symbol? _____

  _____

- Explain in words what the equation shows. _____

  _____

©Curriculum Associates, LLC   Copying is not permitted.

🔍 Find Out More

The equation uses numbers and symbols to describe what the picture shows. In order to solve the problem, you must solve the equation. This means that you need to find the value of the unknown.

$$438 + (4 \times 8) = T$$
$$438 + 32 = T \quad \longleftarrow \text{Always do the operation inside the parentheses first.}$$
$$470 = T \quad \longleftarrow \text{Then do the operation outside the parentheses.}$$

The Shirt Shack will have 470 T-shirts in stock.

Does this answer seem reasonable? You can always use estimation or mental math to check.

Estimation:

$$438 + 32 = T$$
$$440 + 30 = T \quad \longleftarrow \text{Round each number to the nearest 10.}$$
$$440 + 30 = 470 \quad \longleftarrow \text{Add the rounded numbers.}$$

Mental math:

$$438 + 32 = T$$
$$438 + 2 + 30 = T \quad \longleftarrow \text{Change 32 to } 2 + 30.$$
$$440 + 30 = T \quad \longleftarrow \text{Add the 2 to 438 because 440 is easier to work with.}$$
$$440 + 30 = 470 \quad \longleftarrow \text{Add the new numbers.}$$

✏️ Reflect

1 Show and explain how to solve the equation $S = 114 - (2 \times 8)$.

_____

_____

Read the problem below. Then explore different ways to model and solve two-step word problems.

> Third graders at Brown Elementary School are raising money for the school library. The goal is to make $250. They raised $9 each day for 8 days in a row. How much more money is needed to make the goal?

Picture It

You can use a diagram to show a two-step word problem.

```
|————————————————— 250 —————————————————|
| 9 | 9 | 9 | 9 | 9 | 9 | 9 | 9 |              X              |
```

Model It

Use the diagram above to help write an equation for a two-step word problem.

The total amount is $250.

The model shows 8 days at $9 each day, or 8×9.

The oval is the unknown. X added to 8×9 is equal to 250.

Put it all together in an equation: $250 = (8 \times 9) + X$.

©Curriculum Associates, LLC   Copying is not permitted.

🔍 Connect It

Now you will solve the problem from the previous page by modeling and solving the equation.

$$250 = (8 \times 9) + X$$
$$250 = 72 + X$$
$$250 - 72 = X$$
$$X = 178$$

2 What operation is done first? _____ Why? _____

3 Describe in words what $250 = 72 + X$ means. _____

4 Why do you subtract 72 from 250 to find X?

_____

_____

5 What is X and what does it stand for? _____

_____

6 Explain how you can use addition to check your answer. _____

_____

✏️ Try It

Use what you just learned to solve these two-step word problems. Show your work on a separate piece of paper.

7 Tim is saving money to buy a pair of hockey skates that cost $289. For the past 6 weeks, he has saved $7 each week. How much money does Tim have left to save?

_____

8 Nima is training for a bike race. During the first three weeks in April she rode 176 miles. During the last week in April, she rode 9 miles each day for 7 days. How many total miles did Nima ride in April?

_____

Read the problem below. Then explore different ways to estimate solutions to two-step word problems.

Tiny the elephant eats a lot of food during busy weekends at the zoo. One Saturday, Tiny ate 152 pounds of food. On Sunday he ate 12 more pounds of food than he did on Saturday. How many pounds of food did Tiny eat that weekend?

🔍 Picture It

You can use a table to show the information in a two-step word problem.

Amount of Food Tiny Ate	
Saturday	Sunday
152 pounds	152 pounds + 12 pounds

$152 + 152 + 12 = F$

🔍 Model It

Estimate the solution to the two-step problem.

You can round each number to the nearest 100 and add.

152 rounds to 200

12 rounds to 0

$200 + 200 + 0 = 400$

You can also round each number to the nearest 10 and add.

152 rounds to 150

12 rounds to 10

$150 + 150 + 10 = 310$

©Curriculum Associates, LLC   Copying is not permitted.

Connect It

Now you will model and solve the equation from the previous page.

$$152 + (152 + 12) = X$$
$$152 + 164 = X$$

9 You can add in any order. Add the numbers in parentheses. Use numbers that are easy to work with: $150 + 2 + 10 + 2 = $ _____

10 What is the next step? Explain and show it.

_____

11 Compare the solution to the estimates on the previous page. Are they close?

_____

12 Do you think your answer is reasonable? Explain why.

_____

_____

13 Explain how estimation is useful when solving two-step equations.

_____

_____

Try It

Use what you just learned to solve these two-step word problems. Show your work on a separate piece of paper.

14 Joan earned $136 last week and $215 this week. She used some of her earnings to buy a jacket. Joan had $273 left after buying the jacket. How much did she spend on the jacket? _____

15 A bookstore had 650 copies of a new book. The first day, 281 copies were sold. At the end of the week there were only 43 copies left. How many books were sold between the first day and the end of the week?

_____

©Curriculum Associates, LLC   Copying is not permitted.

Study the model below. Then solve problems 16–18.

Student Model

The student uses a bar model to show the 105 strawberries already packed. 5 × B shows how many more bags can be made.

Bridget is packing strawberries in sandwich bags to sell at her gymnastics meet. She has 140 strawberries, and she makes bags of 5. So far Bridget has packed 105 strawberries. How many more bags of 5 strawberries can Bridget make?

Look at how you could show your work using a diagram.

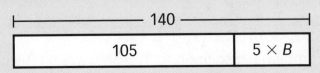

$$105 + (5 \times B) = 140$$

$$5 \times B = 35$$

$$B = 7$$

Solution: ___7 more bags___

Pair/Share

Can you write a different equation to solve this problem?

16 Students earn 1 point for each page they read. A student who earns 300 points gets a no-homework pass. Elise read 8 pages a day for 7 days in a row. How many more points does she need to get a no-homework pass?

Show your work.

What operation do you use to find how many pages Elise has already read?

Pair/Share

How can you check your answer?

Solution: _____

©Curriculum Associates, LLC   Copying is not permitted.

17 Troy scored 945 points playing 3 games of pinball. He scored 312 points in the first game and 354 points in the second game. How many points did Troy score in the third game?

Show your work.

Will you round the numbers to the nearest 10 or 100 to estimate?

🗨**Pair/Share**

Can you solve this problem in a different way?

Solution: _____

18 In the morning, 134 books were checked out of the library. In the afternoon and evening, 254 and 118 books were checked out. How many total books were checked out from the library that day?

A 270

B 388

C 496

D 506

Paolo chose **B** as the correct answer. How did he get that answer?

_____

_____

_____

How can you estimate the answer?

🗨**Pair/Share**

How can you tell if Paolo's answer is reasonable?

Solve the problems.

1 Which equation can NOT be used to solve this problem?

Rosa and Brett are the only two people in a school election. Rosa got 314 votes in the election. She got 18 more votes than Brett. How many people voted in the election?

A $314 + 314 - 18 = N$

B $N = 314 + 314 - 18$

C $314 - 18 + 314 = N$

D $314 + 314 + 18 = N$

2 George estimated that 800 people voted in the election in problem 1. Which mistake could he have made?

A George rounded 18 down to 10 instead of up to 20.

B George rounded 314 down to 300 instead of up to 400.

C George rounded 314 up to 400 instead of down to 300.

D George rounded 18 up to 20 instead of down to 10.

3 A produce manager unpacks 108 bananas. Some are single bananas. There are also 9 bunches of 4 bananas each.

Choose **all** the expressions that can be used to find the number of single bananas there are.

A $N + (9 \times 4) = 108$

B $9 \times 4 = 108 + N$

C $N - (9 \times 4) = 108$

D $108 - (9 \times 4) = N$

E $N + (9 + 4) = 108$

©Curriculum Associates, LLC   Copying is not permitted.

4 A theater sold 379 tickets to a movie. Of those, 192 were children's tickets. The rest were adult tickets. How many fewer adult tickets were sold than children's tickets?

_____ tickets

5 Greg is packing a book order. He has already packed 3 boxes with 5 books in each box. There are 210 books left to pack. How many books are in the whole order?

Show your work.

Answer There are _____ books in the whole order.

6 Gina wants to estimate the total of 3 bills she has to pay. The bills are for $125, $115, and $138. Gina wants to make sure that she has more than enough money. She wants the estimate to be high. Should she round to the nearest 10 or 100?

Answer Gina should round to the nearest _____ to get a high estimate.

Explain your answer.

_____

_____

_____

 **Self Check** _Go back and see what you can check off on the Self Check on page 95._

Solve the problems.

1 A school ordered 36 books for its library. The books came packed in 4 cartons, with an equal number of books in each carton. Which drawing can be used to find the number of books in each carton?

A

B

C

D

2 Jessie bought a number of DVDs for $8 each. She also bought a T-shirt for $12. Jessie spent a total of $84. Which equation can be used to find the number of DVDs that she bought?

A $8 \times D + 12 = 84$

B $8 \times 12 + D = 84$

C $8 + 12 \times D = 84$

D $(8 + 12) \times D = 84$

3 Bianca has 40 books. She decides to put them in a bookcase with 6 shelves. She put the same number of books on each shelf and has 4 books left over. In the picture below, draw the number of books she put on each shelf.

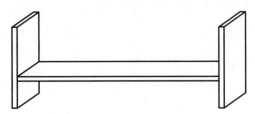

4 Henry worked for 2 hours. Connor worked for 8 hours. They each earned $10 per hour. How much more money did Connor earn than Henry?

$_____ more

©Curriculum Associates, LLC   Copying is not permitted.

5 There are 23 tables in the library. Each table has 4 chairs. Third graders fill the chairs at 3 tables. Fourth graders fill the chairs at 6 tables. The rest of the chairs are empty.

Part A

The letter C stands for the number of chairs with students sitting in them. Write an equation that will help you find C.

Equation _____

Part B

Solve the equation to find the number of chairs with students sitting in them.

Answer _____ chairs with students sitting in them

6 Bev's school put on three music shows. Bev sold 289 tickets for the first show, 115 tickets for the second show, and 198 tickets for the third show.

Part A

How many tickets did Bev sell for all three shows?

Show your work.

Answer _____ tickets

Part B

Explain how you could estimate to find out if your answer is reasonable.

_____

_____

©Curriculum Associates, LLC   Copying is not permitted.

Performance Task

Answer the questions and show all your work on separate paper.

Mr. Perennial is tending to his vegetable garden. His plants are planted in 6 rows with 5 plants in each row. Each plant needs 2 ounces of fertilizer on the day it is planted. One week later he will use a total of 8 ounces of fertilizer for all of the plants.

Draw a picture of Mr. Perennial's garden. How many total ounces of fertilizer will he need for his garden? Write and solve one equation to find your answer.

Mr. Perennial has two 20-ounce containers of fertilizer. How much more does he need to buy? Write and solve one equation to find your answer.

<table>
<tr><td>✓ CHECKLIST</td></tr>
<tr><td>Did you . . .</td></tr>
<tr><td>☐ Draw a diagram?</td></tr>
<tr><td>☐ Use an unknown?</td></tr>
<tr><td>☐ Check your
calculations?</td></tr>
</table>

Reflect on Mathematical Practices

After you complete the task, choose one of the following questions to answer.

1. **Persevere** Which words helped you decide to use multiplication to solve this problem?

2. **Use Structure** How could you find the total number of plants in Mr. Perennial's garden using addition? How could you find the total number of plants using multiplication?

©Curriculum Associates, LLC   Copying is not permitted.

Unit 4
Number and Operations—Fractions

Can you imagine what it would be like if you could only order a whole pizza when you were hungry for only one slice? What if math class had to last a whole hour because no one knew what to call 45 minutes? Fractions are an important part of your everyday life. One slice of a large pizza is $\frac{1}{8}$ of the pizza. Forty-five minutes is $\frac{3}{4}$ of an hour. One fourth of a dollar is— you guessed it—a quarter!

In this unit, you will write fractions and compare fractions. You will also learn to recognize when two fractions are the same.

✓ Self Check

Before starting this unit, check off the skills you know below. As you complete each lesson, see how many more you can check off!

I can:	Before this unit	After this unit
use a fraction to show equal parts of a whole, for example: when a whole has 4 equal parts, each part is $\frac{1}{4}$ of the whole.	☐	☐
use a number line to show fractions and find a fraction on a number line.	☐	☐
understand equivalent fractions, for example: $\frac{1}{3} = \frac{2}{6}$ because they show the same amount.	☐	☐
find equivalent fractions, for example: fractions equivalent to $\frac{1}{2}$ include $\frac{2}{4}, \frac{3}{6}$, and $\frac{4}{8}$.	☐	☐
write whole numbers as fractions, for example: $5 = \frac{5}{1}$ or $\frac{10}{2}$.	☐	☐
compare fractions when they have same-sized wholes using $<, >,$ and $=$, for example: $\frac{1}{3} > \frac{1}{8}, \frac{4}{6} < \frac{5}{6}$, and $\frac{2}{3} = \frac{4}{6}$.	☐	☐

©Curriculum Associates, LLC   Copying is not permitted.

Lesson 14   Part 1: Introduction

Understand What a Fraction Is

How can we describe equal parts?

Fractions are numbers that tell about equal parts of a whole. A fraction is named by the number of equal parts. One of three equal parts is one third. One of four equal parts is one fourth, and so on.

There are two parts to a fraction. The number on the bottom is called the **denominator**. It tells how many equal parts are in the whole.

The number on the top is called the **numerator**. It tells how many equal parts you have or how many are shaded.

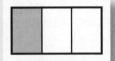

$$\frac{1 \text{ part shaded}}{3 \text{ equal parts in the whole}}$$

🔍 **Think**   Fractions always show equal parts.

All the parts of a whole must be the same size. Think about sharing a cake with some friends. You cut the cake into pieces that are the same so that it is fair.

Circle the model that shows equal parts.

There are 6 equal parts. These are sixths. Each part is $\frac{1}{6}$.

These are not sixths. The parts are not the same size.

©Curriculum Associates, LLC   Copying is not permitted.

🔍 **Think** Unit fractions help us understand other fractions.

A **unit fraction** has a 1 in the numerator. $\frac{1}{4}$ is a unit fraction. It names 1 part of a whole that has 4 equal parts.

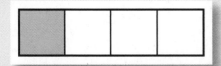

You can count unit fractions like you count whole numbers. Instead of 1, 2, 3, it is $\frac{1}{4}$, $\frac{2}{4}$, $\frac{3}{4}$.

If you know the name of 1 part of the whole, you can count to name more parts of that whole.

Look at the rectangle below. It has 4 equal parts. Each part is $\frac{1}{4}$. The rectangle has three parts shaded. If you put three $\frac{1}{4}$s together, you get $\frac{3}{4}$.

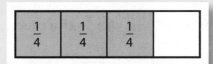

When you count the shaded parts of this rectangle, you say: one fourth, two fourths, three fourths.

You can describe the whole rectangle by counting the number of $\frac{1}{4}$s. There are four $\frac{1}{4}$s in the rectangle, or $\frac{4}{4}$.

| $\frac{1}{4}$ | $\frac{1}{4}$ | $\frac{1}{4}$ | $\frac{1}{4}$ |

✏️ **Reflect**

1 Mike draws a large rectangle. He wants to color $\frac{3}{8}$ of the rectangle blue. How many equal parts should he make? What fraction names each part? How many parts should he color?

_____

_____

_____

🔍 Explore It

You can use models to help you think about fractions.

2   How many equal parts are there? _____

How many parts are shaded? _____

Write the fraction that names the shaded parts. _____

Circle how you would say this fraction: one half   one third   one fourth

3   How many equal parts are there? _____

How many parts are shaded? _____

Write the fraction that names the shaded parts. _____

Circle how you would say this fraction: three halves   three thirds   three fourths

For problems 4 and 5, first write the unit fraction shown. Then shade the given number. Write a fraction for the shaded model.

4

Unit fraction: _____

Shade 2 sections:

What fraction did you shade? _____

5

Unit fraction: _____

Shade 6 sections.

What fraction did you shade? _____

For problems 6–8, write the fraction shown. The parts in each model are all equal.

6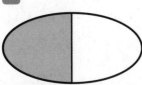

Fraction: _____

7

Fraction: _____

8

Fraction: _____

©Curriculum Associates, LLC   Copying is not permitted.

💬 Talk About It

Solve the problems below as a group.

9 Look at your answers to problems 4 and 5. Explain how you figured out what the unit fraction was in each model. _____

_____

_____

Explain how you figured out the fractions that you shaded. _____

_____

_____

Do you think it matters which of the parts you shaded in each model? Explain.

_____

_____

_____

10 Look at the rectangle below.

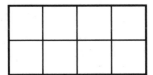

What unit fraction does each part show? _____ Now shade $\frac{4}{8}$ of the rectangle.

✏️ Try It Another Way

Work with your group to use the pictures to draw the correct fraction.

11 This model shows $\frac{1}{3}$ of a square.

Draw what $\frac{2}{3}$ of the square looks like.

12 This model shows $\frac{1}{6}$ of a shape.

Draw what $\frac{3}{6}$ of the shape looks like.

Connect It

Talk through these problems as a class, then write your answers below.

13 Create: This is $\frac{1}{6}$ of a rectangle. Draw a model to show what the whole rectangle might look like.

14 Explain: Look at the squares below. Each square is divided into equal parts.

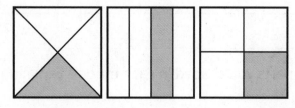

Lynn says each square has the same fraction shaded. Rose says each square has a different fraction shaded. Explain who is correct and why.

_____

_____

_____

15 Compare: Look at the triangles below. Each triangle is divided into equal parts.

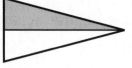

What is the same about the fractions that are shaded in each model?

_____

_____

What is different? _____

_____

©Curriculum Associates, LLC   Copying is not permitted.

Put It Together

16 Use what you have learned to complete this task.

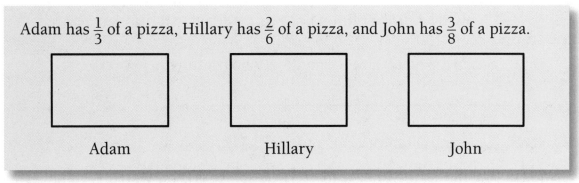

Adam has $\frac{1}{3}$ of a pizza, Hillary has $\frac{2}{6}$ of a pizza, and John has $\frac{3}{8}$ of a pizza.

Adam   Hillary   John

A Show the correct number of equal parts in each pizza. Then shade each pizza to show the fraction each person has.

B Circle one of the pizzas. Explain how you knew what to divide it into and how many parts to shade.

_____

_____

_____

©Curriculum Associates, LLC   Copying is not permitted.

Lesson 15   Part 1: Introduction

Understand Fractions on a Number Line

CCSS
3.NF.A.2a
3.NF.A.2b

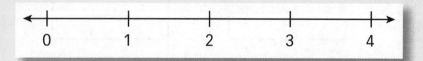

How do number lines help us understand numbers?

You are used to seeing a number line show whole numbers.

$$0 \quad 1 \quad 2 \quad 3 \quad 4$$

Numbers are the same distance apart. The distance is like 1 whole. Each time you add another whole, you count another whole number on the number line.

| 1 whole | 1 whole | 1 whole | 1 whole |

$$0 \quad 1 \quad 2 \quad 3 \quad 4$$

🔍 **Think**   You can show more than just whole numbers on a number line.

Fractions show equal parts of a whole. You can see this on a number line too.

The section between 0 and 1 on a number line shows 1 whole. If you divide this section equally, it is like dividing a whole into equal parts.

> **Underline the sentence that tells why each part of the number line shows $\frac{1}{4}$.**

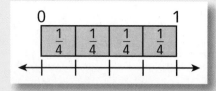

The section between 0 and 1 is divided into 4 equal parts, so each part shows $\frac{1}{4}$.

©Curriculum Associates, LLC   Copying is not permitted.

🔍 **Think** You can figure out what fraction a point on the number line shows.

You can count fractions on a number line just like you can count whole numbers.

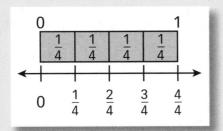

When you count whole numbers, you say 1, 2, 3, 4... When you count fourths, you say $\frac{1}{4}, \frac{2}{4}, \frac{3}{4}, \frac{4}{4}$...

You can also use number lines to show fractions greater than 1.

All you have to do is divide each section between a pair of whole numbers (like 0 and 1 and 1 and 2), into the same number of equal parts. Then just keep counting the fractions.

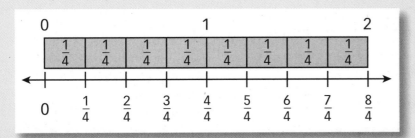

✏️ **Reflect**

1 How many $\frac{1}{3}$s or "thirds" are there between 0 and 1 on a number line? How do you know?

_____

_____

_____

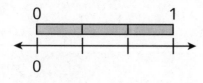

Looking at the number of equal parts helps you think about fractions on a number line.

2   Look at the section between 0 and 1 on the number line.

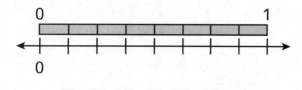

How many equal parts are there? _____

What fraction does each part show? _____

Label the number line with the correct fractions.

3   Look at the section between 0 and 1 on the number line.

How many equal parts are there? _____

What fraction does each part show? _____

Label the number line with the correct fractions.

4   Look at the section between 0 and 1 on the number line.

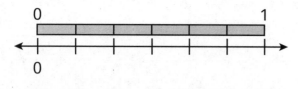

How many equal parts are there? _____

What fraction does each part show? _____

Label the number line with the correct fractions.

©Curriculum Associates, LLC   Copying is not permitted.

💬 Talk About It

Solve the problems below as a group.

5 Look at the number lines in problems 2–4. How is showing fractions on a number line like showing fractions using models? _____

_____

6 Look at the sections between the whole numbers on the number line.

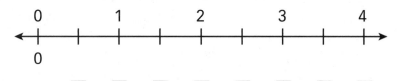

How many equal parts are in each section? _____

What fraction does each part show? _____

Each mark on the number line represents a fraction. What denominator will the fractions have? _____

Label the number line with the correct fractions.

7 Look at the fractions that are greater than 1. What do you notice about the numerator and denominator in each of these fractions? _____

_____

✏️ Try It Another Way

Work with your group to identify the fraction shown.

8 What fraction is at point *A*? _____

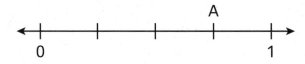

9 What fraction is at point *B*? _____

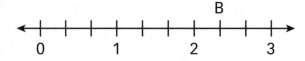

©Curriculum Associates, LLC   Copying is not permitted.

🔍 Connect It

Talk through these problems as a class, then write your answers below.

10 Explain: Look at the number line below.

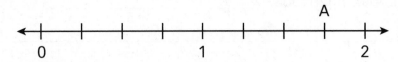

Amira says that point A shows $\frac{7}{8}$. Is she right? Explain why or why not.

_____

_____

_____

_____

11 Demonstrate: Use the number line below to show the fraction $\frac{4}{6}$.

Explain how you knew where to put $\frac{4}{6}$.

_____

_____

_____

12 Illustrate: Use the number line below to show that there are $\frac{8}{8}$ in 1 whole.

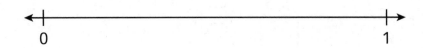

©Curriculum Associates, LLC   Copying is not permitted.

Put It Together

13 Use what you have learned to complete this task.

> Zara and John are hiking on a trail that is 2 miles long. There are signs to mark each eighth of a mile along the trail.

A Draw a number line to show the length of the trail and the location of each sign.

B Zara stopped for water at the $\frac{3}{8}$-mile sign. Label the $\frac{3}{8}$ mark with a **Z** for Zara.

C John stopped to rest after $\frac{12}{8}$ miles. Label the $\frac{12}{8}$ mark with a **J** for John.

D Who stopped before the 1-mile mark? Who stopped after the 1-mile mark? Explain how you know.

_____

_____

_____

_____

_____

©Curriculum Associates, LLC   Copying is not permitted.

Lesson 16   Part 1: Introduction

Understand Equivalent Fractions

CCSS
3.NF.A.3a

How can two different fractions be equal?

Two fractions can be equal if they show the same amount of the whole.

These are called **equivalent fractions**. The same area in each of the circles is shaded. Each circle is divided into a different number of parts. So, the fractions used to name the parts are different.

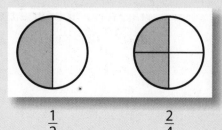

$\frac{1}{2}$ $\frac{2}{4}$

You can also see equivalent fractions using a number line. $\frac{1}{2}$ and $\frac{2}{4}$ are located at the same point on the number line. This shows they are equivalent.

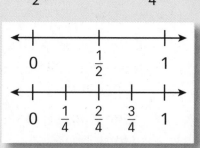

🔍 **Think**   To find equivalent fractions, the size of the wholes must be the same.

The rectangles below are the same size. They show that $\frac{1}{2}$ and $\frac{2}{4}$ are equivalent.

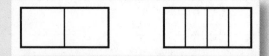

Shade the parts of the first two rectangles that show that $\frac{1}{2}$ and $\frac{2}{4}$ are equivalent.

The rectangles below are not the same size. They show that $\frac{1}{2}$ of a small rectangle is not equivalent to $\frac{2}{4}$ of a large one.

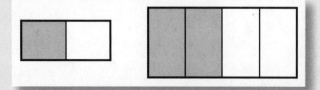

©Curriculum Associates, LLC   Copying is not permitted.

🔍 **Think** It takes more than one smaller part to equal a bigger part.

Once you make sure the wholes are the same size, you can look at the size of the parts in each whole.

$\frac{1}{2}$	$\frac{1}{2}$

$\frac{1}{4}$	$\frac{1}{4}$	$\frac{1}{4}$	$\frac{1}{4}$

Each part is $\frac{1}{2}$. Each part is $\frac{1}{4}$.

To cover the same amount as $\frac{1}{2}$, you need two $\frac{1}{4}$s.

Remember, two $\frac{1}{4}$s are the same as $\frac{2}{4}$, three $\frac{1}{6}$s are the same as $\frac{3}{6}$, and four $\frac{1}{8}$s are the same as $\frac{4}{8}$.

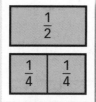

You can also divide the rectangle in different ways to find other fractions that are equivalent to $\frac{1}{2}$.

$\frac{1}{2}$	$\frac{1}{2}$

$\frac{1}{6}$	$\frac{1}{6}$	$\frac{1}{6}$	$\frac{1}{6}$	$\frac{1}{6}$	$\frac{1}{6}$

$\frac{1}{8}$	$\frac{1}{8}$	$\frac{1}{8}$	$\frac{1}{8}$	$\frac{1}{8}$	$\frac{1}{8}$	$\frac{1}{8}$	$\frac{1}{8}$

To cover the same amount as $\frac{1}{2}$, you could also use three $\frac{1}{6}$s or four $\frac{1}{8}$s.

So, $\frac{1}{2}$ is equivalent to $\frac{2}{4}$, $\frac{3}{6}$, and $\frac{4}{8}$.

✏️ **Reflect**

1 Explain why it takes more $\frac{1}{8}$s than $\frac{1}{4}$s to make a fraction equivalent to $\frac{1}{2}$.

_____

_____

_____

Explore It

Models and numbers lines are two ways to show equivalent fractions.

2 Count the equal parts in each model. Then write the correct unit fraction in each section of both models.

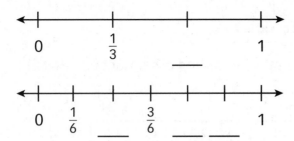

How many $\frac{1}{6}$ s does it take to cover the same amount as $\frac{1}{3}$? _____

How many $\frac{1}{6}$ s does it take to cover the same amount as two $\frac{1}{3}$ s? _____

3 Fill in the missing fractions on each number line.

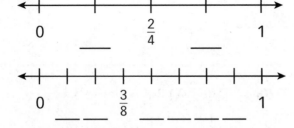

Use the models and number lines above to answer question 4.

4 Write the equivalent fractions: $\frac{1}{3}$ = _____ $\frac{2}{3}$ = _____

Now try these problems.

5 Fill in the missing fractions on each number line.

What fraction is at the same place on the number line as $\frac{1}{4}$? _____

What fraction is at the same place on the number line as $\frac{6}{8}$? _____

6 Write the equivalent fractions: $\frac{1}{4}$ = _____ $\frac{6}{8}$ = _____

©Curriculum Associates, LLC   Copying is not permitted.

💬 Talk About It

Solve the problems below as a group.

7 How is using number lines like using models to find equivalent fractions?

_____

_____

What is different about using number lines and using models to find equivalent fractions?

_____

_____

_____

8 Mila thinks $\frac{1}{2}$ is equivalent to $\frac{2}{3}$ and $\frac{3}{6}$. Label the number lines below and use them to explain whether or not Mila is correct.

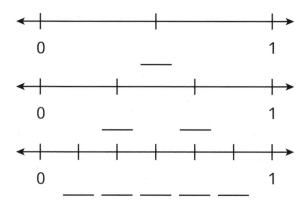

_____

_____

_____

_____

_____

✏️ Try It Another Way

Work with your group to use the fraction strips to show equivalent fractions.

9 Shade a fraction equivalent to $\frac{2}{3}$.

$\frac{1}{3}$	$\frac{1}{3}$	$\frac{1}{3}$

$\frac{1}{6}$	$\frac{1}{6}$	$\frac{1}{6}$	$\frac{1}{6}$	$\frac{1}{6}$	$\frac{1}{6}$

What fraction did you shade? _____

10 Shade a fraction equivalent to $\frac{4}{8}$.

$\frac{1}{6}$	$\frac{1}{6}$	$\frac{1}{6}$	$\frac{1}{6}$	$\frac{1}{6}$	$\frac{1}{6}$

$\frac{1}{8}$	$\frac{1}{8}$	$\frac{1}{8}$	$\frac{1}{8}$	$\frac{1}{8}$	$\frac{1}{8}$	$\frac{1}{8}$	$\frac{1}{8}$

What fraction did you shade? _____

©Curriculum Associates, LLC   Copying is not permitted.

Connect It

Talk through these problems as a class, then write your answers below.

11 **Demonstrate:** Use the fraction strips below to show $\frac{1}{4} = \frac{2}{8}$.

12 **Explain:** Cooper used the models below to show $\frac{2}{3} = \frac{2}{6}$. What did Cooper do wrong?

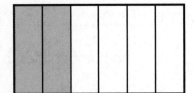

_____

_____

_____

13 **Illustrate:** The number line below shows $\frac{1}{2}$. Add marks to show eighths. Above the number line, label the fractions you added to the number line.

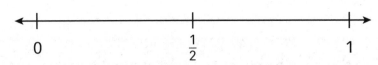

What fraction is equivalent to $\frac{1}{2}$? _____

©Curriculum Associates, LLC   Copying is not permitted.

Put It Together

14 Use what you have learned to complete this task.

Four friends each ate a part of their own granola bar. All the granola bars were the same size. The table below shows how much of a granola bar each friend ate.

Friend	Part of Granola Bar Eaten
Meg	$\frac{4}{6}$
Joe	$\frac{4}{8}$
Beth	$\frac{6}{8}$
Amy	$\frac{2}{3}$

A Which two friends ate the same amount? Draw models to show that your answer is correct. Circle the names of the two children who ate the same amount.

B Fred also had a granola bar. He divided it into fourths. He ate the same amount as Beth. Draw two number lines to show what fraction of his granola bar Fred ate.

What fraction of his granola bar did Fred eat? _____

©Curriculum Associates, LLC   Copying is not permitted.

Lesson 17   Part 1: Introduction

Find Equivalent Fractions

CCSS

3.NF.A.3b
3.NF.A.3c

In Lesson 16, you learned that equivalent fractions tell about the same amount of the whole. Take a look at this problem.

Izzy's mom baked a cake. She put chocolate frosting on half of the cake and vanilla frosting on half of the cake.

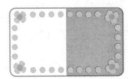

Then Izzy's mom cut the cake into fourths. What is a different fraction that names the part of the cake that has chocolate frosting?

 Explore It

Use the math you already know to solve the problem.

- Look at the picture above. What fraction of the cake has chocolate frosting?

  _____

- How many equal parts should the cake be divided into to show fourths? _____

- On the picture above, draw lines to divide the cake into fourths.

- How many fourths of the cake have chocolate frosting? _____

- Did the amount of cake with chocolate frosting change? Explain how you know that $\frac{1}{2}$ of the cake is the same as $\frac{2}{4}$.

  _____

  _____

  _____

©Curriculum Associates, LLC   Copying is not permitted.

🔍 Find Out More

In the last lesson, you looked at stacked models to understand equivalent fractions. Both models were the same size, but divided into a different number of equal parts. You looked for fractions that named the same amount of the whole.

You can also find equivalent fractions by dividing the same model in different ways. The cake already showed $\frac{1}{2}$. You may have drawn lines in one of these ways to show fourths.

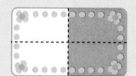 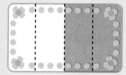 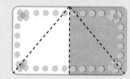

No matter how the fourths are made, the models show that $\frac{2}{4}$ of the cake has chocolate frosting.

You can also divide a number line in different ways to show that $\frac{1}{2}$ is equivalent to $\frac{2}{4}$.

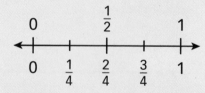

✏️ Reflect

1 Izzy's mom now wants to cut the cake into eighths. Explain how to figure out how many eighths of the cake have chocolate frosting.

_____

_____

_____

©Curriculum Associates, LLC   Copying is not permitted.

Read the problem below. Then explore different ways to think about equivalent fractions.

Casen ate $\frac{2}{8}$ of an orange. Trey's orange is the same size. He ate $\frac{1}{4}$ of it. Show that the two boys ate the same amount.

Picture It

You can use models to help find equivalent fractions.

This model shows $\frac{2}{8}$.   This model shows $\frac{1}{4}$.

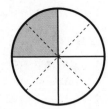   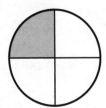

Look at the model of $\frac{2}{8}$. The solid lines show the division into fourths. The dotted lines show how each fourth was divided to make eighths.

Model It

You can also use a number line to help find equivalent fractions.

This number line shows both fourths and eighths.

©Curriculum Associates, LLC   Copying is not permitted.

💡 Connect It

Now you will solve the problem from the previous page using equations.

2 How do you know that $\frac{2}{8}$ of the first model are shaded? _____

_____

3 How do you know that $\frac{1}{4}$ of the second model is shaded? _____

_____

4 Explain how the models show that the fractions are equivalent. _____

_____

5 How does the number line show that the fractions are equivalent? _____

_____

6 Write sentences to show the fractions of the two oranges name the same amount.

use words: Two eighths is equal to _____.

use fractions: _____ equals _____.

7 Explain how you can show two fractions are equivalent. _____

_____

_____

✏️ Try It

Use what you just learned to solve these problems.

8 Draw a model to show $\frac{2}{3} = \frac{4}{6}$.

9 Use the number line to find a fraction equivalent to $\frac{1}{3}$.

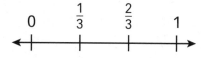

Read the problem below. Then explore different ways to write a whole number as a fraction.

> Kacey used 2 same-sized boards to build a birdhouse. He cut each board into fourths. How can you write 2 as a fraction to show Kacey's boards divided into fourths?

Picture It

You can use models to help you write a whole number as a fraction.

The fraction strips below show 2 wholes, each divided into fourths.

$\frac{1}{4}$	$\frac{1}{4}$	$\frac{1}{4}$	$\frac{1}{4}$

$\frac{1}{4}$	$\frac{1}{4}$	$\frac{1}{4}$	$\frac{1}{4}$

Each part is $\frac{1}{4}$ of a whole. There are eight $\frac{1}{4}$s in all.

Model It

You can use a number line to help you write a whole number as a fraction.

This number line shows whole numbers on the top and fourths on the bottom.

```
0                 1                 2
+---+---+---+---+---+---+---+---+--->
0   1   2   3   4   5   6   7   8
    4   4   4   4   4   4   4   4
```

Notice that each whole number has an equivalent fraction.

©Curriculum Associates, LLC   Copying is not permitted.

Connect It

Now you will solve the problem from the previous page using equations.

10 Look at the models on the previous page. How many equal parts are in 1 whole?

Explain how you know. _____

_____

_____

11 How many parts are in 2 wholes? Explain how you know. _____

_____

_____

12 Write sentences to show the fraction that is equivalent to 2.

use words: Two wholes equals _____.

use a fraction: 2 equals _____.

13 Explain how to find a fraction equivalent to a whole number.

_____

_____

_____

Try It

Use what you just learned to solve these problems.

14 Use the model to find a fraction equivalent to 3.

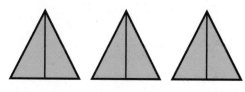

3 = _____

15 Draw a model to show $3 = \frac{18}{6}$.

Read the problem. Then explore different ways to write a whole number as a fraction with a denominator of 1.

> Justin picked 4 green peppers from his garden. He did not cut them into pieces. How can you write 4 as a fraction to show Justin's green peppers?

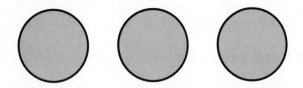 **Picture It**

You can use models to help you write a whole number as a fraction with a denominator of 1.

Each circle stands for 1 green pepper.

They are not divided into pieces, so each whole is made of one part.

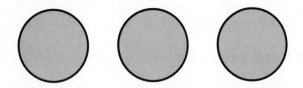 **Model It**

You can use a number line to help you write a whole number as a fraction with a denominator of 1.

This number line shows whole numbers on the top and fractions on the bottom.

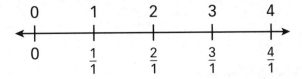

Notice that each whole number has an equivalent fraction. The spaces between whole numbers are not divided into parts. Each whole number is made of one part, so the denominator is 1.

©Curriculum Associates, LLC   Copying is not permitted.

Connect It

Now you will solve the problem from the previous page.

16 Explain how you know each whole only has 1 part. _____

_____

17 How many parts do the 4 green peppers make? _____

18 What does the numerator of a fraction show? _____

19 What does the denominator of a fraction show? _____

_____

20 Write a fraction equivalent to 4.

$\left(\text{Remember: } \dfrac{\text{number of parts}}{\text{number of equal parts in a whole}}\right)$ _____

21 Explain how to write a whole number as a fraction with a denominator of 1. Why does this work?

_____

_____

_____

Try It

Use what you just learned to solve these problems.

22 Use the model to find a fraction equivalent to 6.

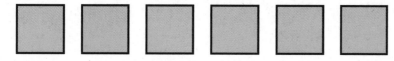

6 = _____

23 Draw a model to show $5 = \frac{5}{1}$.

The student used solid lines to show fourths and dotted lines to show eighths.

Study the model below. Then solve problems 24–26.

Student Model

Caleb and Hannah bought two melons that are the same size. Caleb cut his into fourths. Hannah cut hers into eighths. Hannah ate $\frac{4}{8}$ of her melon, and Caleb ate an equal amount of his melon. What fraction did Caleb eat?

Look at how you could show your work using a model.

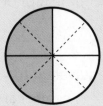

Solution: _Caleb ate $\frac{2}{4}$ of his melon._

💬Pair/Share

How could you solve this problem using a number line?

How many thirds are in 1 whole? How many eighths are in 1 whole?

24. Matt says $\frac{3}{3}$ is equivalent to 1. Elisa says $\frac{8}{8}$ is equivalent to 1. Who is correct?

Show your work.

💬Pair/Share

What is another fraction that is equivalent to 1?

Solution: _____

©Curriculum Associates, LLC   Copying is not permitted.

25 Show two fractions that are equivalent to 5.

Show your work.

> There will be 5 wholes in all. Think about how many parts will be in each whole.

Solution: _____

Pair/Share

How did you decide what denominators to use in your fractions?

26 Kaia ate $\frac{3}{6}$ of a banana. Zoie ate an equivalent amount. Which fraction shows how much Zoie ate? Circle the letter of the correct answer.

A $\frac{1}{3}$

B $\frac{2}{3}$

C $\frac{5}{8}$

D $\frac{1}{2}$

Landon chose **A** as the correct answer. How did he get that answer?

_____

_____

> Look at where $\frac{3}{6}$ is on a number line. What other fraction could be shown at the same point?

Pair/Share

Does Landon's answer make sense?

Solve the problems.

1   Which fraction shown is equivalent to $\frac{2}{6}$?

A   **B**   **C**   **D**

2   Which fraction is equivalent to 3?

A $\frac{3}{1}$

B $\frac{1}{3}$

C $\frac{4}{1}$

D $\frac{6}{3}$

3   Look at point *P* on the number line.

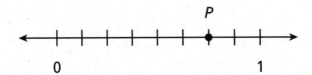

Look at number lines 3a–3c. Is the point on each number line equal to the number shown by point *P*? Choose *Yes* or *No*.

a. ☐ Yes   ☐ No

b. ☐ Yes   ☐ No

c. ☐ Yes   ☐ No

©Curriculum Associates, LLC   Copying is not permitted.

4 For numbers 4a–4d, choose *Yes* or *No* to indicate whether each number graphed on the number line represents one whole.

a.

$$0 \quad \frac{1}{1} \quad \frac{2}{1} \quad \frac{3}{1} \quad \frac{4}{1}$$

☐ Yes ☐ No

b.

$$0 \quad \frac{1}{1} \quad \frac{2}{1} \quad \frac{3}{1} \quad \frac{4}{1}$$

☐ Yes ☐ No

c.

$$0 \quad \frac{1}{4} \quad \frac{2}{4} \quad \frac{3}{4} \quad 1$$

☐ Yes ☐ No

d.

$$0 \quad \frac{1}{4} \quad \frac{2}{4} \quad \frac{3}{4} \quad \frac{4}{4}$$

☐ Yes ☐ No

5 Use the number line below to find a fraction equivalent to 3.

Show your work.

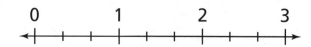

$$0 \qquad 1 \qquad 2 \qquad 3$$

Answer 3 is equivalent to _____

6 Draw a model to find a fraction equivalent to $\frac{1}{4}$.

Show your work.

Answer $\frac{1}{4}$ is equivalent to _____

✓ **Self Check** *Go back and see what you can check off on the Self Check on page 131.*

©Curriculum Associates, LLC   Copying is not permitted.

Lesson 18   Part 1: Introduction

Understand Comparing Fractions

CCSS
3.NF.A.3d

How do we compare fractions?

When you compare fractions, you figure out which is smaller, which is larger, or if they are the same size.

You can use models or number lines to help you compare two fractions.

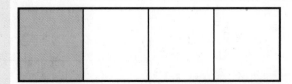

Both of these show that $\frac{1}{4}$ is less than $\frac{2}{4}$.

The size of the wholes must be the same to compare fractions. If not, it might look like $\frac{1}{4}$ is greater than $\frac{2}{4}$.

🔍 **Think**   Sometimes when you compare fractions, the denominators are the same.

The models below show two wholes that are the same size divided into sixths.

Circle the model of the fraction that is less.

Think about how many unit fractions it takes to make each fraction you are comparing.

It takes two $\frac{1}{6}$s to make $\frac{2}{6}$.   It takes five $\frac{1}{6}$s to make $\frac{5}{6}$.

$\frac{2}{6}$ is made of fewer unit fractions than $\frac{5}{6}$. So, $\frac{2}{6}$ is less than $\frac{5}{6}$.

©Curriculum Associates, LLC   Copying is not permitted.

🔍 **Think** You can compare fractions with like numerators and different denominators.

Think about two different unit fractions from the same whole, such as $\frac{1}{3}$ and $\frac{1}{8}$.

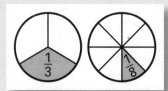

Compare the denominators of $\frac{1}{3}$ and $\frac{1}{8}$. 3 is less than 8, so the whole is divided into fewer parts. Since there are fewer parts, each part is bigger. So, the unit fraction $\frac{1}{3}$ is greater than $\frac{1}{8}$.

It's like cutting up a piece of paper. The more pieces you cut the paper into, the smaller each piece is.

Here's another example:

| $\frac{1}{6}$ | $\frac{1}{6}$ | $\frac{1}{6}$ | | | |

| $\frac{1}{4}$ | $\frac{1}{4}$ | $\frac{1}{4}$ | |

The unit fractions used to make $\frac{3}{6}$ are smaller.

The unit fractions used to make $\frac{3}{4}$ are bigger.

3 smaller parts are less than 3 bigger parts. So, $\frac{3}{6}$ is less than $\frac{3}{4}$.

✏️ **Reflect**

1 Explain how you can use unit fractions to help you compare fractions.

_____

_____

_____

_____

©Curriculum Associates, LLC   Copying is not permitted.

Explore It

Use the models to help you compare fractions with the same denominator.

2 Write the fraction shaded below each model. Circle the fraction that is greater.

_____   _____

3 Write the fraction shaded below the first model. Shade the second model to show a greater fraction. Write the greater fraction.

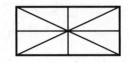

_____   _____

Use the models to help you compare fractions with the same numerator.

4 Write the fraction shaded below each model. Circle the fraction that is greater.

_____   _____

5 Write the fraction shaded below each model. Circle the fraction that is less.

_____   _____

6 Write the fraction shaded below the first model. Shade the second model to show a fraction that is less but has the same numerator.

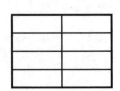

_____

Explain how you know the fraction is less. _____

_____

_____

©Curriculum Associates, LLC   Copying is not permitted.

Talk About It

Solve the problems below as a group.

7 Look at your answers to problems 2 and 3. Explain how to use unit fractions to compare fractions with the same denominator. _____

_____

_____

8 Look at your answers to problems 4–6. What is different about the numerators and denominators in these fractions than the fractions in problems 2 and 3?

_____

_____

Explain how to use unit fractions to compare the fractions with the same numerator. _____

_____

_____

9 Isaiah is comparing $\frac{3}{8}$ and $\frac{3}{6}$. Both fractions have a numerator of 3. How can he tell which fraction is less? _____

_____

_____

Try It Another Way

Work with your group to use the number lines to compare fractions.

10 Look at the fractions on the number lines. Circle the fraction that is less.

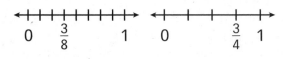

11 Look at the fractions on the number lines. Circle the fraction that is greater.

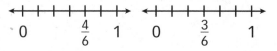

🔍 Connect It

Talk through these problem as a class, then write your answers below.

12 Create: Draw an area model or number line to show $\frac{5}{8}$. Find a fraction with the same denominator that is less than $\frac{5}{8}$.

Explain how you found your answer. _____

_____

13 Explain: Mario painted $\frac{2}{6}$ of the wall in his bedroom. Mei Lyn painted $\frac{2}{4}$ of a wall in her bedroom. Both walls are the same size. Explain how you know who painted

more. _____

_____

_____

14 Justify: Jace and Lianna each baked a loaf of bread. Jace cut his in halves and Lianna cut hers in thirds.

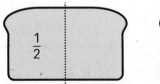 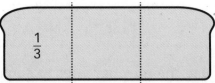

Jace says they can use their loaves of bread to show that $\frac{1}{2}$ is less than $\frac{1}{3}$. Lianna says they can't. Who is correct? Explain why. _____

_____

_____

©Curriculum Associates, LLC   Copying is not permitted.

Put It Together

15

Mrs. Ericson made sandwiches for her 4 children. Each sandwich was the same size. After lunch, each child had a different fraction of his or her sandwich left. Matt had $\frac{1}{4}$, Elisa had $\frac{3}{8}$, Carl had $\frac{3}{4}$, and Riley had $\frac{7}{8}$.

A Use this information to write a problem that compares two fractions with the same numerator. _____

_____

B Use this information to write a problem that compares two fractions with the same denominator. _____

_____

C Choose one of your problems to solve. Circle the question you chose. Draw a model or number line to help you find the answer.

Explain how you could use unit fractions to think about the problem.

_____

_____

_____

Lesson 19   Part 1: Introduction 👥

Use Symbols to Compare Fractions

In Lesson 18, you learned how to compare fractions. Take a look at this problem.

Erica's cup is $\frac{4}{6}$ full. Ethan's cup is $\frac{5}{6}$ full. Use $<$, $>$, or $=$ to compare $\frac{4}{6}$ and $\frac{5}{6}$.

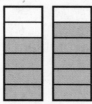

🔍 Explore It

Use the math you already know to solve the problem.

- The fractions have the same denominator. What do you need to think about to compare the two fractions? _____

  _____

  _____

- How many sixths does Erica have? _____

- How many sixths does Ethan have? _____

- Use a symbol to compare those two whole numbers. _____

- Is the amount in Erica's cup less than, greater than, or equal to the amount in Ethan's' cup? _____

- Explain how you can use a symbol to compare the two fractions. _____

  _____

©Curriculum Associates, LLC   Copying is not permitted.

Find Out More

You have already learned how to figure out if one fraction is less than, greater than, or equal to another. Now you will use the symbols $<$, $>$, or $=$ to compare fractions.

$<$ means less than $>$ means greater than $=$ means equal to

Think of the $<$ and $>$ symbols as the mouth of an alligator. The alligator's mouth will always be open to eat the greater fraction.

Think about the fractions $\frac{1}{2}$ and $\frac{1}{8}$. $\frac{1}{2}$ is greater. $\frac{1}{8}$ is less.

 or

$\frac{1}{2}$ is greater than $\frac{1}{8}$ or $\frac{1}{8}$ is less than $\frac{1}{2}$.

You can switch the order of the fractions. Just be careful which symbol you use. If the greater fraction is first, you use $>$. If the greater fraction is last, you use $<$.

Also, remember that sometimes one fraction is not greater than the other. Sometimes they are equivalent. Then you use $=$ to compare them.

$$\frac{1}{2} = \frac{1}{2} \quad \text{and} \quad \frac{7}{8} = \frac{7}{8}$$

Reflect

1 Use the symbols $<$ and $>$ to compare $\frac{7}{8}$ and $\frac{3}{8}$. Explain your answers.

_____

_____

_____

©Curriculum Associates, LLC   Copying is not permitted.

Read the problem below. Then explore different ways to compare fractions.

Use $<$, $>$, or $=$ to compare $\frac{4}{8}$ and $\frac{4}{6}$.

You can use models to help you compare fractions.

This model shows $\frac{4}{8}$. This model shows $\frac{4}{6}$.

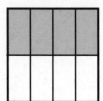 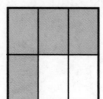

Model It

You can also use number lines to help you compare fractions.

This number line is divided into eighths. It shows $\frac{4}{8}$.

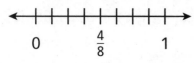

This number line is divided into sixths. It shows $\frac{4}{6}$.

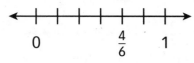

©Curriculum Associates, LLC   Copying is not permitted.

Connect It

Now you will solve the problem from the previous page using symbols.

2 Explain how you can use the model to compare the fractions.

_____

_____

3 Explain how you can use the number lines to show how the fractions compare.

_____

4 Write the comparison:

using words: 4 eighths is _____ than 4 sixths.

using symbols: $\frac{4}{8}$ _____ $\frac{4}{6}$

5 Now switch the order of the fractions. Write the comparison:

using words: 4 sixths is _____ than 4 eighths.

using symbols: $\frac{4}{6}$ _____ $\frac{4}{8}$

6 Explain how to use symbols to compare two fractions.

_____

_____

_____

Try It

Use what you just learned about using symbols to compare fractions to solve these problems. You can draw models on a separate piece of paper.

7 Use <, >, or = to compare each set of fractions. Each symbol will be used once.

$\frac{4}{6}$ _____ $\frac{2}{6}$ $\frac{2}{4}$ _____ $\frac{2}{3}$ $\frac{1}{2}$ _____ $\frac{1}{2}$

8 Use <, >, or = to compare each set of fractions. Each symbol will be used once.

$\frac{3}{4}$ _____ $\frac{3}{4}$ $\frac{2}{8}$ _____ $\frac{2}{2}$ $\frac{2}{3}$ _____ $\frac{1}{3}$

©Curriculum Associates, LLC   Copying is not permitted.

Study the models below. Then solve problems 9–11.

The fractions have the same denominator, so they are easy to compare on the same number line.

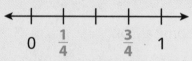
Student Model

Su and Anthony live the same distance from school. Su biked $\frac{3}{4}$ of the way to school. In the same amount of time, Anthony walked $\frac{1}{4}$ of the way to school. Who went the greater distance? Compare the fractions using a symbol.

Look at how you could show your work using a number line.

```
←——+——+——+——+——+——→
   0   1/4     3/4  1
```

Solution: <u>Su went a greater distance. $\frac{3}{4} > \frac{1}{4}$</u>

Pair/Share

How do you find the greater number on a number line?

What do you need to think about when you compare fractions that have different denominators?

9 Julia and Mackenzie have the same number of homework problems. Julia has done $\frac{1}{3}$ of her problems. Mackenzie has done $\frac{1}{2}$ of her problems. Which student has done less of her homework? Compare the fractions using a symbol.

Show your work.

Pair/Share

How did you know which fraction was smaller?

Solution: _____

©Curriculum Associates, LLC   Copying is not permitted.

10 David and Rob each got the same snack pack of crackers. David ate $\frac{3}{6}$ of his snack pack. Rob ate $\frac{3}{4}$ of his snack pack. Who ate more? Compare the fractions using a symbol.

Show your work.

I think drawing a model might help. Be sure the wholes are the same size.

Solution: _____

Pair/Share

Which fraction is made of bigger unit fractions? Why?

11 What number could go in the blank to make the comparison true? Circle the letter of the correct answer.

$$\frac{5}{8} < \underline{\hspace{2cm}}$$

A $\frac{5}{8}$

B $\frac{4}{8}$

C $\frac{6}{8}$

D $\frac{1}{8}$

Blake chose **A** as the correct answer. How did he get that answer?

_____

_____

_____

Is $\frac{5}{8}$ less than or greater than the fraction that goes in the blank?

Pair/Share

Does Blake's answer make sense?

Solve the problems.

1 Which fraction could go in the blank to make the comparison true?

$$\underline{\hspace{2cm}} > \frac{1}{2}$$

A $\frac{2}{4}$

B $\frac{4}{8}$

C $\frac{2}{3}$

D $\frac{2}{6}$

2 Shade the rectangles below to represent the given fractions. Then use your diagrams to help you complete the statement below with $<$, $>$, or $=$.

$\frac{1}{4}$ [rectangle divided into 4 parts]

$\frac{2}{8}$ [rectangle divided into 8 parts]

$\frac{1}{4}$ ☐ $\frac{2}{8}$

3 Use the numbers below to build fractions that make the statement true. There is more than one correct answer.

6   8   1   3   4

$$\frac{\square}{8} < \frac{\square}{8}$$

©Curriculum Associates, LLC   Copying is not permitted.

4   Look at the comparison below.

$$\underline{\hspace{3cm}} < \frac{3}{4}$$

Tyrone wrote a fraction in the blank to make the comparison true. His fraction had an 8 in the denominator. What is one fraction that Tyrone could have used?

Show your work.

Answer _____

5   Tran and Noah were each given the same amount of clay in art class. Tran divided his clay into 3 equal pieces. He used 2 of the pieces to make a bowl. Noah divided his clay into 4 equal pieces. He also used 2 of the pieces to make a bowl. Tran said that he had more clay left over than Noah. Is Tran correct? Explain.

_____

_____

_____

✓ Self Check   *Go back and see what you can check off on the Self Check on page 131.*

©Curriculum Associates, LLC   Copying is not permitted.

Solve the problems.

1 Which of these shows a fraction that is equal to the fraction modeled below?

A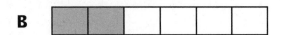

B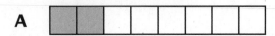

C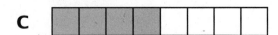

D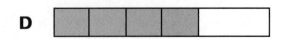

2 Look at the number lines below.

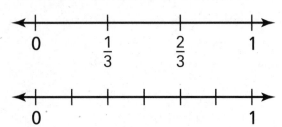

Which fraction is equivalent to $\frac{1}{3}$?

A $\frac{1}{6}$ **C** $\frac{4}{6}$

B $\frac{2}{6}$ **D** $\frac{5}{6}$

3 Fill in each box with the fraction below that matches the location on the number line.

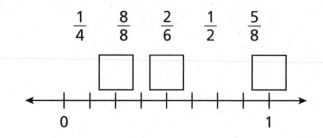

4 Choose **all** the fractions that are equivalent to 2.

A $\frac{1}{2}$ **D** $\frac{4}{2}$

B $\frac{2}{1}$ **E** $\frac{2}{4}$

C $\frac{2}{2}$

5 Which sentences are false? Circle the letter for all that apply.

A Two fractions cannot be equivalent if they have different denominators.

B A fraction that has the same number in both the numerator and denominator is equal to 1.

C A fraction with the number 1 in the denominator is called a unit fraction.

D All fractions are less than 1.

©Curriculum Associates, LLC   Copying is not permitted.

6

Part A

Draw 3 lines to divide the number line below into 4 equal sections. Label each line with the correct fraction.

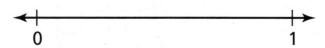

Part B

What fraction does each section in Part A represent?

Answer _____

7 The pictures below show Mark's backyard and Jamal's backyard. Each boy wants to use $\frac{1}{2}$ of his backyard for a garden.

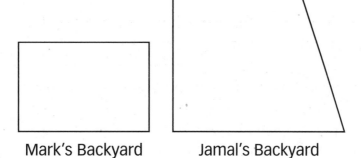

Mark's Backyard   Jamal's Backyard

Will the two gardens be the same size? Explain why or why not.

_____

_____

_____

©Curriculum Associates, LLC   Copying is not permitted.

Performance Task

Answer the questions and show all your work on separate paper.

The owner of the neighborhood pizzeria, **Itsa Pizza**, would like you to make pictures to hang in her restaurant. Each picture will show a rectangular pizza cut into eight equal-sized pieces with different combinations of toppings. She wants each pizza to be completely covered with toppings with no overlaps. Use grid paper to sketch pictures of the pizzas described below. If the toppings won't fully cover the pizza, add a new topping or change the amounts of the toppings shown. If the instructions list too many toppings, change the amounts of the toppings to make it work.

An example is shown.

Peppers & Roni	$\frac{1}{2}$ pepper, $\frac{1}{2}$ pepperoni

P	P	P	P
R	R	R	R

P = pepper
R = pepperoni

Deluxe	$\frac{1}{8}$ mushroom, $\frac{3}{8}$ olive, $\frac{1}{4}$ broccoli, $\frac{1}{4}$ sausage
Onion-Roni	$\frac{5}{8}$ pepperoni, $\frac{1}{8}$ onion, $\frac{1}{8}$ sausage
Veggie D-lite	$\frac{1}{2}$ pepper, $\frac{2}{8}$ broccoli, $\frac{1}{4}$ mushroom
The Itsa Pizza	$\frac{2}{4}$ tomato, $\frac{1}{4}$ olive
Mighty Meaty	$\frac{1}{4}$ sausage, $\frac{4}{8}$ pepperoni, $\frac{2}{4}$ hamburger
The Green Hula	$\frac{3}{4}$ onion, $\frac{3}{3}$ pineapple, $\frac{1}{4}$ broccoli

CHECKLIST

Did you . . .

☐ Sketch each pizza?

☐ Provide a key?

☐ Check your calculations?

Reflect on Mathematical Practices

After you complete the task, choose one of the following questions to answer.

1. **Model** How did you decide how much of the pizza to cover with what toppings?

2. **Reason Mathematically** How many different fractions listed in the pizza descriptions were ways to show half a pizza?

©Curriculum Associates, LLC   Copying is not permitted.

Unit 5
Measurement and Data

What time does the movie start? How far is it to the basketball court? How much do those apples weigh? How much milk do I need for the pancake recipe? How many tiles do I need to tile that floor? The answers to these questions are all examples of different types of measurements.

In this unit, you will learn to choose the right kind of measurement for different situations. You will also gather information about groups of items and compare them and organize the information with graphs.

✓ Self Check

Before starting this unit, check off the skills you know below. As you complete each lesson, see how many more you can check off!

I can:	Before this unit	After this unit
tell and write time on digital clocks and clocks with hands and solve problems about time.	☐	☐
estimate liquid volume and solve problems about liquid volume.	☐	☐
estimate mass and solve problems about mass.	☐	☐
solve problems using pictographs and bar graphs.	☐	☐
draw pictographs and bar graphs to show data.	☐	☐
measure lengths and show data on a line plot.	☐	☐
understand area, find areas by multiplying, and add areas.	☐	☐
add to find perimeters and find shapes with the same perimeter and different areas or the same area and different perimeters.	☐	☐

©Curriculum Associates, LLC   Copying is not permitted.

Lesson 20   Part 1: Introduction 👥

Tell and Write Time

CCSS
3.MD.A.1

In this lesson, you will tell time to the minute. Take a look at this problem.

Lily started reading a book at the time shown on the clock.

What time does the clock show?

🔍 Explore It

Use the math you already know to solve the problem.

■ The short hand shows the hour. What number did the short hand go past?
_____

■ The long hand shows the minutes. What number did the long hand go past?
_____

■ You can count by fives to help you figure out the minutes. Each mark is 1 minute. If the long hand is on the 6, how many minutes past 8 is it? _____

■ The long hand is 2 small marks past the six. Explain how you can find the time shown on the clock. _____

_____

_____

©Curriculum Associates, LLC   Copying is not permitted.

Find Out More

On a clock the short hand shows the hour. It takes 1 hour for the short hand to move from one number to the next.

The long hand shows the minutes. There are 60 minutes in 1 hour. Each small mark on the clock shows 1 minute. It takes 5 minutes for the long hand to move from one number to the next.

Since the short hand has gone past the 8 (and isn't to the 9 yet), the hour is 8.

To find the minutes, start at the 12. Then count by fives until you get to the 6. The long hand is 2 small marks past the 6, so count 2 more to get to 32. It is 8:32.

You could also figure out the minutes another way. Multiply 6 by 5 (because each number shows 5 minutes) and then add 2.

A digital clock like this one has a way to show what part of the day it is. AM starts at midnight and ends at noon. PM starts at noon and ends at midnight.

Reflect

1 Sometimes a clock does not have numbers at all. It only has the small marks and large marks. Explain how you can tell what time this clock shows.

_____

_____

_____

Read the problem below. Then explore different ways to tell and write time.

Sara sat down to eat lunch at 43 minutes past noon. At what time did she sit down to eat lunch?

🔍 Picture It

You can use a digital clock to show what time it is.

Noon is 12:00 PM. Sara sat down at 43 minutes past noon.

. The clock shows 12:43. It shows PM because the time is between noon and midnight.

🔍 Solve It

You can use the next hour to tell what time it is.

Sara sat down to eat between 12:00 and 1:00. You can tell the time by saying how many minutes after 12:00. You can also say how many minutes before 1:00.

To count the minutes, you always start at the 12. Count forward to find out how many minutes after 12:00. Count backward from the 12 to find out how many minutes before 1:00.

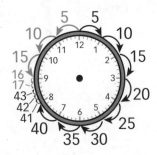

By counting backward, you can see that 43 minutes after 12:00 is the same as 17 minutes before 1:00.

Sara sat down to eat at 17 minutes before 1:00.

©Curriculum Associates, LLC   Copying is not permitted.

✎ Connect It

Now you will show the time from the problem on the previous page by drawing the hands on a clock.

2 Which hand on a clock shows the hour? _____

What number should this hand go past? _____

Explain how you know the hour. _____

3 Which hand on a clock shows the minutes? _____

How many minutes should this hand show? _____

4 At what time did Sara sit down to eat? _____

5 Draw the hands on the clock to show what time Sara sat down to eat.

6 Explain how to tell time to the minute on a clock with hands.

_____

_____

✎ Try It

Use what you just learned to solve these problems.

7 Write the time in two ways.

_____

_____ minutes before _____

8 It is 7 minutes before 2 PM. Write the time and draw the hands on the clock to show the time. _____

Study the model below. Then solve problems 9–11.

Student Model

Jen used a clock to help count backwards from the 12 to find the number of minutes before the next hour.

Jen woke up at the time shown on the clock. What time did she wake up? Give your answer in minutes before the next hour.

Look at how you could show your work using a clock.

Solution: _18 minutes before 7:00_____

💬**Pair/Share**

How else could you solve the problem?

💬**Pair/Share**

What two numbers would the hour be between? What two numbers would 24 minutes be between?

9 Ezra started working in the garden at the time shown on the clock.

Draw the hands to show what the time looks like on this clock.

💬**Pair/Share**

How did you and your partner know where to draw each hand?

©Curriculum Associates, LLC   Copying is not permitted.

10 Abby's piano lesson started at the time shown on the clock.

Fill in the correct time on the digital clock. Be sure to show whether it is AM or PM.

> *Think about what Abby is doing. Would she most likely have a piano lesson when it is AM or PM?*

⊙Pair/Share

What is something else you might be doing at the time shown?

11 Luca started cleaning his room at the time shown on the clock.

Which correctly tells about the time shown on the clock? Circle the letter of the correct answer.

A 9 minutes before 9:00

B 9 minutes before 10:00

C 11 minutes before 10:00

D 51 minutes before 9:00

Bo chose **D** as the correct answer. How did he get that answer?

_____

_____

> *All of the choices tell the time before the hour. What do you need to do to figure that out?*

⊙Pair/Share

Does Bo's answer make sense?

Solve the problems.

1 Which pair of clocks shows the same time?

A

C

B

D

2 Which phrases describe the time shown on the clock? Circle the letter for all that apply.

A   48 minutes after 5:00

B   48 minutes before 5:00

C   48 minutes before 6:00

D   12 minutes before 5:00

E   12 minutes before 6:00

F   12 minutes after 6:00

©Curriculum Associates, LLC   Copying is not permitted.

3 Adam started baseball practice at the time shown on the clock.

Draw the hour and minute hands on the clock below to show the time that baseball practice started.

4 Ruby left to go swimming this morning at the time shown on the clock.

Write the time on the digital clock below. Be sure to mark AM or PM. Then tell the time before the hour. Show your work.

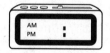

Answer Ruby left _____ minutes before _____.

✓ **Self Check** *Go back and see what you can check off on the Self Check on page 179.*

Lesson 21   Part 1: Introduction

Solve Problems About Time

CCSS
3.MD.A.1.

In Lesson 20, you learned how to tell time to the minute. Take a look at this problem.

Beth left her house at 4:30. She arrived at dance class at 5:05. How long did it take Beth to get to dance class from her house?

🔍 Explore It

Use the math you already know to solve this problem.

▪ Draw the hands on the two clocks below to show the correct times.

Left house   **Arrived at dance class**

▪ Look at the first clock. How many minutes before 5:00 is 4:30? _____

▪ Look at the second clock. How many minutes after 5:00 is 5:05? _____

▪ Explain how you can find the total amount of time it took Beth to get from her house to dance class. _____

_____

©Curriculum Associates, LLC   Copying is not permitted.

🔍 Find Out More

Elapsed time is the time that has passed between a starting time and an ending time. To find elapsed time, you can count the number of minutes between the starting time and the ending time. You can use a clock to help you.

At 4:30, the long hand is on the 6. At 5:05, the long hand is on the 1.

In this problem, the starting time and ending time are in different hours on the clock. Beth left her house at 4:30. She arrived at dance class at 5:05. You can figure out how many minutes before 5:00 she left (30 minutes) and how many minutes after 5:00 she arrived (5 minutes). Then you can add these amounts: 30 + 5 = 35.

You can also use a number line to help you understand elapsed time. Each long mark shows 5 minutes. Count minutes on the number line just like you would on a clock.

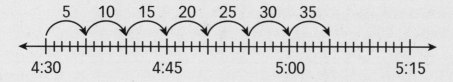

✏️ Reflect

1 Elsa started eating lunch at 11:25 and finished at 11:45. Explain how to find out how long it took Elsa to eat lunch. _____

_____

_____

_____

©Curriculum Associates, LLC   Copying is not permitted.

Read the problem below. Then explore different ways to find the end time when you know the start time and the amount of elapsed time.

> Jenna got home from school at 3:30. She did math homework for 10 minutes. Then she did science homework for 15 minutes. Then she practiced the piano for 22 minutes. What time did Jenna finish?

Picture It

You can use a clock to help you find the end time.

The first clock shows 3:30, since that is when Jenna started her homework. 10 minutes are counted for her math homework, 15 minutes for her science homework, and 22 minutes for her piano practice.

The second clock shows the time Jenna finished.

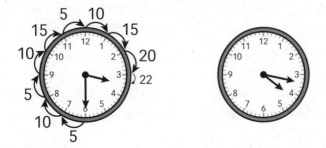

Model It

You can also use a number line to help you find the end time.

This number line shows times instead of ordinary numbers. Each long mark shows 5 minutes.

Start at 3:30. Jump along the number line three times to show how long it took Jenna to do each thing.

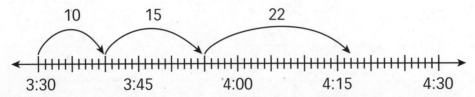

The last jump on the number line shows what time Jenna was finished with all three things.

©Curriculum Associates, LLC   Copying is not permitted.

Connect It

Now you will find the end time for the problem from the previous page.

2 Explain how to figure out how many total minutes Jenna spent doing homework and practicing piano. _____

3 Explain how you could use the total elapsed time to find what time Jenna finished doing her homework and practicing the piano. _____

_____

4 What time did Jenna finish? _____ Why is the hour not 3 anymore?

_____

_____

5 Explain how to find the ending time when you know the start time and the total elapsed time. _____

_____

_____

_____

Try It

Use what you have learned about finding the end time to help you solve these problems.

6 Nate finished supper at 7:10. He did dishes for 15 minutes and then took a shower for 10 minutes. Then he read for 15 minutes before he went to bed. What time did Nate go to bed? _____

7 Kari started talking on the phone at 5:45. She talked to her grandma for 10 minutes, her grandpa for 5 minutes, and her cousin for 8 minutes. What time did Kari get off the phone? _____

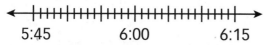

5:45   6:00   6:15

Read the problem below. Then explore different ways to find the start time when you know the end time and the amount of elapsed time.

> Marc's guitar lesson starts at 4:20. It takes 15 minutes to get there from his house, and before he leaves, he has to do some chores for 25 minutes. What time should Marc start doing his chores to make it to his lesson on time?

🔍 Picture It

You can use a clock to help you find the start time.

The clock shows 4:20, since that is when Marc's guitar lesson starts. 15 minutes are counted backward for the time it takes to get to his lesson, and 25 minutes are counted backward for the time it will take to do his chores.

The second clock shows the time Marc should start his chores.

🔍 Model It

You can also use a number line to help you find the start time.

This number line is like the one used for the last problem. It shows times, and each long mark shows 5 minutes. Each short mark shows 1 minute.

Start where 4:20 would be.

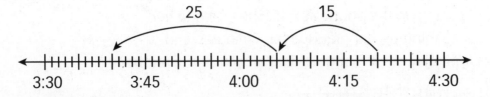

Count backward the time it will take to get to his lesson and do his chores.

©Curriculum Associates, LLC   Copying is not permitted.

Connect It

Now you will find the start time for the problem from the previous page.

8 Explain why the times are counted backward on the clock and the number line.

_____

_____

9 What time should Marc start doing his chores? _____

Why is the hour not 4 anymore? _____

_____

10 Explain how to find the starting time when you know the end time and the elapsed time. _____

_____

_____

Try It

Use what you've learned about finding the start time to help you solve these problems.

11 Enrique walked 5 minutes from his grandma's house to the store, stopped at the store for 20 minutes, and then walked 10 minutes from the store to his house. He got home at 6:00. What time did he leave his grandma's house? _____

12 Mira finished helping make lunch at 12:30. She cut up fruit for 10 minutes and made sandwiches for 7 minutes. What time did she start helping? _____

12:00   12:15   12:30   12:45   1:00

©Curriculum Associates, LLC   Copying is not permitted.

Study the model below. Then solve problems 13–15.

The student used what she knew about telling time before and after the hour to find the answer.

Student Model

Malea's soccer game started at 9:40 and ended at 10:32. How long was Malea's game?

Look at how you could show your work.

9:40 is 20 minutes before 10:00.

10:32 is 32 minutes after 10:00.

20 + 32 = 52

Solution: _____52 minutes_____

Pair/Share

How else could you have solved this problem?

Do you need to count minutes forward or backward from 2:15 to find the time he started watching his sister?

13 Lamar watched his little sister while his mom was busy. He played blocks with her for 15 minutes, peek-a-boo for 5 minutes, and trains for 13 minutes. His mom came back to put her down for a nap at 2:15. What time did Lamar start watching his sister?

Show your work.

Pair/Share

How did you decide how you would solve the problem?

Solution: _____

©Curriculum Associates, LLC   Copying is not permitted.

14 Mr. Chen started doing yard work at 10:00. He watered flowers for 6 minutes, weeded his garden for 12 minutes, and trimmed bushes for 27 minutes. What time was Mr. Chen done with his yard work?

Show your work.

I think adding all of the times together would make this problem easier to solve.

Solution: _____

Pair/Share
Did you need to draw a clock or number line to help you? Why or why not?

15 Carter finished cleaning his room at 11:35. It took him 10 minutes to put all his toys away and 4 minutes to make his bed. What time did Carter start cleaning his room? Circle the letter of the correct answer.

A 11:49

B 11:25

C 11:21

D 10:21

Ann chose **A** as the correct answer. How did she get that answer?

Will the time Carter started be before or after 11:35?

_____

_____

_____

Pair/Share
Does Ann's answer make sense?

Solve the problems.

1 What is the elapsed time between 1:08 and 1:37?

   A   25 minutes   **C**   30 minutes

   B   29 minutes   **D**   31 minutes

2 It took Juan 5 minutes to ride his bike to the park, where he played basketball for 25 minutes. Then it took him 5 minutes to ride home again. He got home at 10:10. Which clock shows the time Juan left for the park?

A

C

B

D

3 Patty, Joyce, and Stef are getting ready to leave for school. Choose *Yes* or *No* to tell whether each girl will be ready before 7:45.

   a.   Patty gets up at 7:10. It takes her 10 minutes to get ready, 7 minutes to pack her lunch, and 15 minutes to eat breakfast.   ☐ Yes   ☐ No

   b.   Joyce gets up at 6:50 and exercises for 30 minutes. Then it takes her 20 minutes to get ready and 12 minutes to eat breakfast.   ☐ Yes   ☐ No

   c.   Stef gets up at 7:15. It takes her 15 minutes to get ready, 5 minutes to pack her lunch, and 9 minutes to eat breakfast.   ☐ Yes   ☐ No

©Curriculum Associates, LLC   Copying is not permitted.

4 Joe spent 40 minutes reading a magazine. Choose **all** the pairs of clocks that show possible times that he started and finished.

A   Start: Finish:

C   Start: Finish:

B   Start: Finish:

D   Start: Finish:

5 Mariah played two games of checkers with her brother. The first game took 12 minutes and the second game took 18 minutes. They put the game away at 7:55. What time did they start?

Show your work.

Answer They started playing at _____.

6 Seve started writing thank you notes at 5:25. It took him 20 minutes to write them. He also spent some time writing addresses on the envelopes. He finished at 6:00. How long did it take Seve to write the addresses?

Show your work.

Answer It took Seve _____ minutes to write the addresses.

 **Self Check** *Go back and see what you can check off on the Self Check on page 179.*

©Curriculum Associates, LLC   Copying is not permitted.

Lesson 22   Part 1: Introduction 👥

Liquid Volume

In Lessons 20 and 21, you learned about measuring time using a clock. You can also measure liquid volume. Take a look at this problem.

Zeke has a ruler, a measuring cup, a small bucket, and a large bucket. He wants to know how much water each of the two buckets can hold. How can Zeke measure this?

🔍 Explore It

Use the math you already know to solve this problem.

- Think about measuring how tall each bucket is. Explain how you would do this.

  _____

  _____

- Does measuring how tall each bucket is help you know how much water each bucket can hold? Explain why or why not. _____

  _____

  _____

  _____

- What tool could Zeke use to measure the amount of water each bucket can hold?

  _____

- Explain how Zeke could measure the amount of water each bucket can hold.

  _____

  _____

©Curriculum Associates, LLC   Copying is not permitted.

🔍 Find Out More

When you figure out how much water is in a bucket, you measure liquid volume. **Liquid volume** measures the amount of liquid a container can hold.

To measure the amount in each of the buckets, Zeke must use something that holds liquid, like the measuring cup. He could count how many times he fills the measuring cup and pours it into the bucket before the bucket is full.

There are standard units to measure liquid volume. One unit is called a **liter**. You can use a measuring cup or a liter beaker to measure using liters.

It is also helpful to picture about how much a liter is.

the amount of water in a large water bottle   the amount of milk in 4 small milk cartons   the amount of milk in $\frac{1}{4}$ of a gallon

✏️ Reflect

1. Name one container that definitely holds less than a liter, one container that holds about a liter, and one container that definitely holds more than a liter.

_____

_____

©Curriculum Associates, LLC   Copying is not permitted.

Read the problem below. Then explore different ways to estimate to solve a word problem about liquid volume.

Kayla will use a liter beaker to fill her goldfish's small fish tank. Estimate how many liters of water the fish tank can hold.

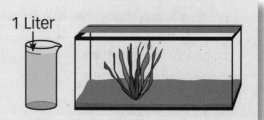

Picture It

You can use a model to help you estimate.

You can picture how many liter beakers would fit inside the fish tank.

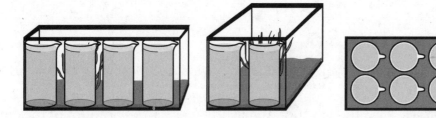

You can count how many beakers fit inside the fish tank. They do not fit perfectly. They do not fill up all the space in the fish tank. So, the number you count will be an estimate.

Model It

You can model the problem in another way to help you estimate.

This shows 1 liter of water in the fish tank.

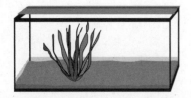

You can think about what fraction of the fish tank is filled when 1 liter is in it.

©Curriculum Associates, LLC   Copying is not permitted.

Connect It

Now you will estimate to solve the problem from the previous page.

2 Look at the water that was poured into the fish tank. Explain how to find the fraction of the fish tank that is filled with 1 liter of water.

_____

_____

3 Explain how you can use this fraction to estimate how many liters the fish tank holds.

_____

_____

4 About how many liters of water will the fish tank hold? _____

5 Now look at the picture of the beakers inside the aquarium. Is your estimate close to the estimate this picture shows? _____

6 Explain how to estimate the number of liters of water it would take to fill a container.

_____

_____

_____

Try It

Use the liter beaker and what you just learned to help you estimate the volume of each container.

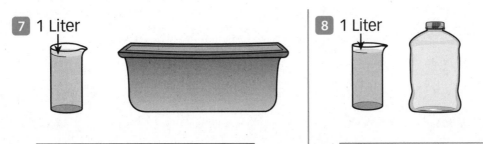

7 1 Liter

_____

8 1 Liter

_____

©Curriculum Associates, LLC   Copying is not permitted.

Read the problem below. Then explore different ways to solve a word problem about liquid volume.

Maria has a cooler full of 8 liters of lemonade. She wants to put it into pitchers to place on the tables at her party. Each pitcher holds 2 liters. How many pitchers will Maria need?

🔍 Picture It

You can use a model to help you solve the problem.

The following model shows the lemonade in the cooler. Each mark on the left side shows 1 liter. Each section shows 2 liters.

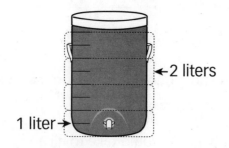

🔍 Model It

You can model the problem in another way to help you solve it.

Each pitcher contains 2 liters. There are 8 liters in all.

©Curriculum Associates, LLC   Copying is not permitted.

Connect It

Now you will solve the problem from the previous page using an equation.

9 How does the picture in the Picture It section show you how many liters of lemonade are in the cooler? _____

_____

How does the picture in the Picture It section show you how many pitchers are needed to hold all the lemonade? _____

_____

_____

10 What do you need to do to find the number of pitchers Maria needs?

_____

_____

11 Write a division equation with an unknown and a multiplication equation with an unknown to show how to solve the problem.

_____

12 Before you have a complete answer, you must add a label to the number. What is the answer to the problem, including the label? _____

Explain why it is important to label your answer. _____

_____

_____

Try It

Use what you just learned to solve these problems.

13 Ginny's sink was full of 10 liters of water. She drained 4 liters out of it. How much water was left in the sink? _____

14 Ethan has 7 jugs of water. Each jug contains 3 liters. How much water does Ethan have altogether? _____

Study the model below. Then solve problems 15–17.

The student wrote a subtraction equation because the question asked about how much was left.

💬**Pair/Share**

How else could you solve this problem?

Student Model

Coach Bond brought 15 liters of water to soccer practice. During practice, the players drank 9 liters. How many liters of water are left?

Look at how you could show your work using an equation.

$$15 - 9 = 6$$

Solution: __6 liters of water left__

How many liters of liquid laundry soap do Jack's mom and Sophie's mom have altogether? The big container must be able to hold that much.

💬**Pair/Share**

What question could you ask that would be solved with a subtraction equation?

15 Jack's mom has a 3-liter bottle of liquid laundry soap. Sophie's mom has a 5-liter bottle of liquid laundry soap. They want to combine the two bottles in one big container. How many liters must the big container be able hold?

Show your work.

Solution: _____

©Curriculum Associates, LLC   Copying is not permitted.

16 Mary poured the juice from a 1-liter bottle into this drink dispenser. Estimate the liquid volume of the drink dispenser.

Solution: _____

17 Jason keeps his turtle in a tank that holds 20 liters of water. He keeps his frog in a tank that holds 10 liters of water. How much greater is the volume of the turtle tank than the frog tank? Circle the letter of the correct answer.

A 2 liters

B 10 liters

C 30 liters

D 200 liters

Maya chose **C** as the correct answer. How did she get that answer?

_____

_____

You could think about how many bottles would fit in the dispenser, or you could look at how full it is after 1 liter is poured in.

💬**Pair/Share**

What strategy did you use to estimate the liquid volume?

You need to find out how much more water is in one tank than in the other. How can you do that?

💬**Pair/Share**

Does Maya's answer make sense?

Solve the problems.

1 The pot below contains 1 liter of water.

Which is the best estimate for how much water the pot could hold?

A 2 liters

B 5 liters

C 10 liters

D 20 liters

2 Noah filled a watering can with 8 liters of water. He used the same amount of water to water each of 4 different flower pots. He used all of the water. How much water did he use for each pot?

A 2 liters

B 6 liters

C 12 liters

D 32 liters

3 Susan buys 10 liters of drinking water. If she drinks one liter a day, how much water will she have left after a week?

_____

©Curriculum Associates, LLC   Copying is not permitted.

4   Choose **all** the containers that hold less than a liter.

     A   kitchen sink

     B   tube of toothpaste

     C   baby food jar

     D   bathtub

     E   paper cup

5   Molly filled a tub for her dog using a 4-liter bucket. She filled the bucket 6 times. How much water did Clara use to wash her dog?

Show your work.

Answer _____ liters

✓ **Self Check**   *Go back and see what you can check off on the Self Check on page 179.*

©Curriculum Associates, LLC   Copying is not permitted.

Lesson 23   Part 1: Introduction 👥

Mass

CCSS
3.MD.A.2

In Lesson 22, you learned about measuring liquid volume. You can also measure mass. Take a look at this problem.

Bristol has a measuring cup, a scale, and a bowl. How can Bristol measure how heavy the bowl is?

🔍 Explore It

Use the math you already know to solve this problem.

▪ Think about measuring the liquid volume of the bowl. Explain how you could do this. _____

_____

_____

▪ What does liquid volume tell you about the bowl? _____

_____

▪ What tool does Bristol have that could be used to measure how heavy the bowl is?

_____

▪ Explain how Bristol could measure how heavy the bowl is. _____

_____

_____

©Curriculum Associates, LLC   Copying is not permitted.

Find Out More

When you measure how heavy something is, you are measuring its **mass**. Two units used to measure mass are **gram** and **kilogram**.

The mass of a paper clip is about 1 gram.

A kilogram has a mass of 1,000 grams. So, it is as heavy as 1,000 paper clips.

The mass of a wooden baseball bat or a large hardcover book also is about a kilogram.

You can use different types of scales to measure mass.

Reflect

1. Elena's brother says the family dog has a mass of 30 grams. Elena says the dog has a mass of 30 kilograms. Who do you think is correct? Why do you think so?

_____

_____

_____

©Curriculum Associates, LLC   Copying is not permitted.

Read the problem below. Then explore different ways to estimate mass.

Jamie bought some flour at the store. Estimate the mass of the bag of flour.

Picture It

You can use models to help you estimate the mass of an object.

Jamie picked up these two books. Then he picked up the bag of flour. They seemed to have about the same mass.

Model It

You can also use a balance scale to help you estimate the mass of an object.

Jamie put the bag of flour on one side of the balance scale and some kilogram and gram weights on the other side.

You can see that it takes about two 1-kilogram weights and three 10-gram weights to balance the scale.

©Curriculum Associates, LLC   Copying is not permitted.

Connect It

Now you will estimate the mass of the bag of flour to solve the problem from the previous page.

2 Explain why Jamie used books instead of paper clips to help him estimate the mass of the bag of flour. _____

_____

3 The mass of each book is about 1 kilogram. What should Jamie estimate for the mass of the bag of flour? Explain why. _____

_____

4 Look at the balance. It shows the actual mass of the bag of flour. What was the actual mass of the bag of flour?

_____

Was your estimate close to the actual mass? _____

_____

5 Explain how to estimate the mass of a plastic cup. _____

_____

_____

_____

Try It

Use what you just learned to solve these problems.

6 Would you estimate the mass of a table using grams or kilograms?

_____

7 Would you estimate the mass of a comic book using grams or kilograms?

_____

©Curriculum Associates, LLC   Copying is not permitted.

Read the problem below. Then explore different ways to solve a word problem about mass.

> Nick has an orange that has a mass of 220 grams and an apple that has a mass of 110 grams. What is the mass of the two pieces of fruit combined?

Picture It

You can use a balance scale to help you solve the problem.

This balance shows the mass of the orange.

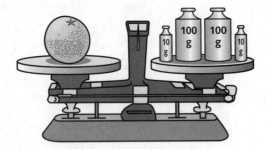

This balance shows the mass of the apple.

This balance shows the mass of the two combined. Both pieces of fruit were placed on one side, and all of the weights were placed on the other side.

©Curriculum Associates, LLC   Copying is not permitted.

Connect It

Now you will use an equation to solve the problem from the previous page.

8　How do you decide which operation to use to solve this problem?

_____

_____

9　What does the picture of the scale show you that could help you solve the
problem? _____

_____

10　Write an equation and solve the problem. _____

_____

11　Explain how you could estimate to know that your answer makes sense.

_____

_____

_____

12　Explain why *grams* has to be part of your answer to this problem.

_____

_____

_____

Try It

Use what you just learned to solve these problems.

13　Jeff had 400 grams of peanuts. He shared them equally between 4 people. How
much did each person get? _____

14　Micah's dog has a mass of 23 kilograms. Nate's dog has a mass of 8 kilograms.
How much heavier is Micah's dog than Nate's dog? _____

©Curriculum Associates, LLC　Copying is not permitted.

Study the problem below. Then solve problems 15–17.

The student wrote a subtraction equation to find the difference between the mass when the suitcase was empty and the mass when it was full.

💬**Pair/Share**

How else could you solve this problem?

Student Model

Jen's suitcase has a mass of 2 kilograms when it is empty. After she packed for her trip, the suitcase was 16 kilograms. What is the mass of the things Jen packed in her suitcase?

Look at how you could show your work using an equation.

$$16 - 2 = 14$$

Solution: ___14 kilograms___

---

15 Ruby's mom bought 4 bags of potatoes. Each bag had a mass of 4 kilograms. What was the total mass of all 4 bags?

Show your work.

There are 4 bags with 4 kilograms of potatoes in each bag. That reminds me of using equal groups.

💬**Pair/Share**

How did you decide which operation to use to solve the problem?

Solution: _____

©Curriculum Associates, LLC   Copying is not permitted.

16 Jane had a sandwich and a banana for lunch. The sandwich's mass was 140 grams. The banana's mass was 130 grams. What is the total mass of the sandwich and the banana?

Show your work.

Solution: _____

Don't forget to label your answer. Are you finding the total mass in grams or kilograms?

Pair/Share

What question could you ask that would use a subtraction equation to solve it?

17 Brock's dad bought a 10-kilogram bag of rice. Then he divided it evenly into 5 smaller bags. How much rice did each smaller bag have in it? Circle the letter of the correct answer.

A 2 kilograms

B 5 kilograms

C 15 kilograms

D 50 kilograms

Felicia chose **D** as the correct answer. How did she get that answer?

_____

_____

_____

Will the amount in each smaller bag be greater or less than 10 kilograms?

Pair/Share

Does Felicia's answer make sense?

©Curriculum Associates, LLC   Copying is not permitted.

Solve the problems.

1 Which is the best estimate for the mass of a watermelon?

    A   30 kilograms

    B   30 grams

    C   3 kilograms

    D   3 grams

2 Which objects have a mass of about a gram? Circle the letter for all that apply.

    A   rubber band

    B   box of crayons

    C   pair of scissors

    D   dollar bill

    E   library book

3 Mrs. Martin is grocery shopping. She has a 4-kilogram bag of flour in her shopping bag. Then she adds some potatoes to her bag. The scale below shows how much the potatoes weigh. How much does her bag weigh, in kg, with both the flour and the potatoes?

_____

©Curriculum Associates, LLC   Copying is not permitted.

4 When Lara was born, her mass was 3 kilograms. By the time she started third grade, she had gained 24 kilograms. What was Lara's mass at the beginning of third grade?

Show your work.

Answer _____ kilograms

5 Margo's soccer coach brought a large bag of watermelons to practice. The mass of the bag with all the watermelons in it was 12 kilograms.

Explain how you could use estimation to figure out about how many watermelons are in the bag.

_____

_____

_____

Estimate the number of watermelons in the bag. Show your work and explain what you did at each step.

Show your work.

Answer There are about _____ watermelons in the bag.

 **Self Check** *Go back and see what you can check off on the Self Check on page 179.*

©Curriculum Associates, LLC Copying is not permitted.

Lesson 24   Part 1: Introduction 👥

Solve Problems Using Scaled Graphs

CCSS
3.MD.B.3

You have had practice modeling and solving word problems. Take a look at this problem.

Ron kept track of the points scored by his teammates during a basketball game. He put his data in a pictograph.

Points Scored During the Game

Alan	🏀
Cate	🏀🏀🏀
Gary	🏀🏀🏀🏀🏀
Mae	🏀🏀🏀🏀

Each 🏀 stands for 2 points

🔍 Explore It

Use the math you already know to solve the problem.

- The sentence at the bottom of the graph tells you that each 🏀 stands for _____ points

- There is 1 🏀 next to Alan's name. That means that Alan scored 2 points. There are 3 🏀 next to Cate's name.

  How many points did Cate score? _____ points

- How many 🏀 are next to Gary's name? _____

- How many points did Gary score? _____ points

- Explain how you could find the number of points Mae scored.

  _____

©Curriculum Associates, LLC   Copying is not permitted.

Find Out More

A **pictograph** uses pictures or symbols to show data. The **key** on a pictograph tells what each symbol stands for.

Look at Ron's pictograph. The key tells us that each 🏀 stands for 2 points. You can multiply the number of 🏀 by 2 to find the total points each student scored.

Student	Number of 🏀	×	Points for each basket	=	Total Points
Alan	1	×	2	=	2
Cate	3	×	2	=	6
Gary	5	×	2	=	10
Mae	4	×	2	=	8

The same basketball data can be shown on a **bar graph**. The bars on the graph show how many points each student scored.

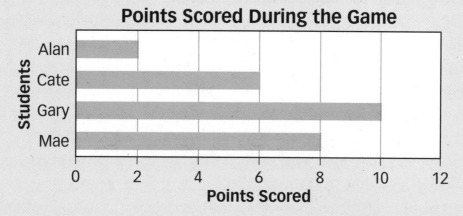

The numbers along the bottom of the bar graph are called the scale. The **scale** marks off equal sections. On this graph the scale counts by 2s.

Reflect

1 What if the key in the pictograph showed that each 🏀 stood for 3 points instead of 2? Explain how you could find the number of points Mae scored.

_____

_____

_____

©Curriculum Associates, LLC   Copying is not permitted.

Read the problem below. Then explore different ways to answer questions about pictographs.

Jaime asked students in his school to choose their favorite season. The pictograph shows how students answered. How many more students chose summer than winter as their favorite season?

Favorite Season

Winter	☺☺☺☺
Spring	☺☺☺
Summer	☺☺☺☺☺☺
Fall	☺☺☺☺☺

Each ☺ stands for 5 students

Picture It

You can use models to understand the problem.

Remember: Each ☺ stands for 5 students.

Model It

You can also use number lines to help understand the problem.

Remember that each ☺ stands for 5 students.

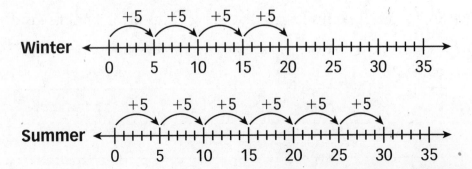

©Curriculum Associates, LLC   Copying is not permitted.

Connect It

Now you will solve the problem from the previous page using number sentences.

2 What does the problem ask you to find?

_____

_____

3 Complete the key. Each 😊 stands for _____ students.

4 Find the number of students who chose winter or chose summer.

Season	Number of 😊	×	Each 😊 stands for	=	Number of Students
Winter	4	×	5	=	_____
Summer	_____	×	5	=	_____

5 Find how many more students chose summer than winter.

$30 - 20 =$ _____

So _____ more students chose summer than winter.

6 Explain why the key is so important when you are solving a problem that has a pictograph.

_____

_____

_____

Try It

Use the graph on the previous page and what you just learned about pictographs to solve these problems. Show your work on a separate sheet of paper.

7 How many students did NOT choose spring or summer? _____

8 How many more students chose spring or fall than summer? _____

Read the problem below. Then explore different ways to answer questions about a bar graph.

The Hart School wants to build a new playground. The graph shows the number of dollars each class has raised to build the playground. How much more money must Grade 3 and Grade 4 raise in order to have $300?

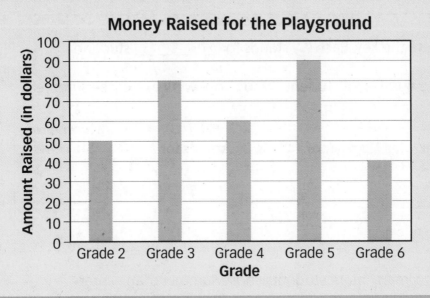

Money Raised for the Playground

Q Model It

You can use words to model how to find each amount on the graph.

Third Grade: Point to the Grade 3 bar. Look at where the bar ends.
Find the number on the left side of the bar graph to tell how much.

Fourth Grade: Point to the Grade 4 bar. Look at where the bar ends.
Find the number on the left side of the bar graph to tell how much.

©Curriculum Associates, LLC   Copying is not permitted.

Connect It

Now you will solve the problem from the previous page using number sentences. Use the bar graph on the previous page to find the answers.

9 What does each bar on this graph show? _____

10 What do the numbers along the left side of the bar graph tell you?

_____

11 By what amount do numbers on the left side of the bar graph change? _____

12 Look at where the Grade 3 bar ends. How much money did Grade 3 raise? _____

Look at where the Grade 4 bar ends. How much money Grade 4 raise? _____

13 What operation should you use to find out how much money was raised by Grade 3 and Grade 4 altogether? _____

How much money did Grade 3 and Grade 4 raise altogether? _____

14 What operation should you use to find out how much more money must be raised in order for the classes to have $300? _____

How much more money must the two classes raise to have $300? _____

15 Explain how the numbers along the edge of a bar graph help you to understand what the bar graph is showing.

_____

_____

Try It

Use the graph on the previous page and what you just learned about bar graphs to solve these problems. Show your work on a separate sheet of paper.

16 How much money in all have the classes raised? _____

17 How much more money have Grade 4 and Grade 5 raised than Grade 2 and Grade 3? _____

©Curriculum Associates, LLC   Copying is not permitted.

Study the model below. Then solve problems 18–20.

Student Model

The student multiplied the number of marker symbols by the key to find the number of markers Ms. Santos bought for each class.

Ms. Santos buys markers for each class. How many more markers does Ms. Santos buy for Grade 3 than for Grade 2?

Markers for Each Class

Grade 2	✏✏✏✏
Grade 3	✏✏✏✏✏✏✏
Grade 4	✏✏✏✏✏✏✏✏
Grade 5	✏✏✏✏✏

Each ✏ stands for 10 markers

Look at how you could show your work using multiplication.

Grade	Number of ✏	×	Each ✏ stands for	=	Number of Markers
Grade 3	7	×	10	=	70
Grade 2	4	×	10	=	40

Solution: ___30 more markers___

Pair/Share

What operation do you use to find how many more markers Ms. Santos bought for Grade 3 than Grade 2?

---

18 Use the graph above to solve this problem. How many markers did Ms. Santos buy altogether?

Show your work.

What steps will you use to solve this problem?

Pair/Share

How else could you solve this problem?

Solution: _____

©Curriculum Associates, LLC   Copying is not permitted.

Use the graph to solve problems 19 and 20.

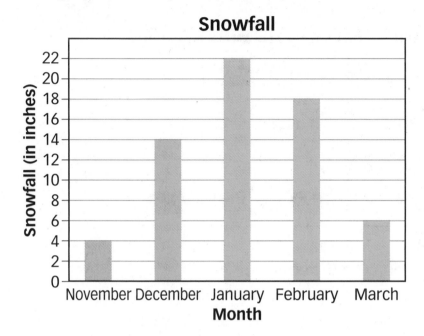

Snowfall

I think there are at least two different steps to this problem.

19 How much more snow fell in February and March than in November and December?

Show your work.

Solution: _____

Pair/Share

What data on the bar graph do you need to solve the problem?

20 Which 2 months have the same amount of snowfall as January? Circle the letter of the correct answer.

A February and March

B December and March

C November and December

D November and February

Lara chose **D** as the correct answer. How did she get the answer?

_____

_____

_____

I think the first step is to find the snowfall for January.

Pair/Share

How did you and your partner decide whether to add or subtract?

Solve the problems.

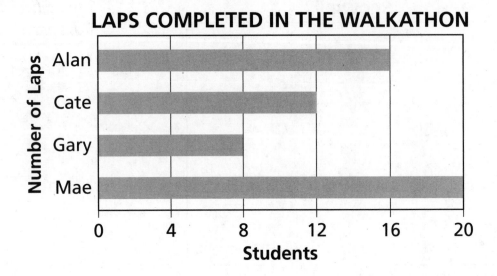

LAPS COMPLETED IN THE WALKATHON

Number of Laps — Alan, Cate, Gary, Mae

Students — 0, 4, 8, 12, 16, 20

1 The graph shows the number of laps each student completed in the walkathon. How many laps in all did the students walk?

A   4

B   14

C   20

D   56

2 How many more laps did Cate and Mae walk than Alan and Gary?

_____ laps

©Curriculum Associates, LLC   Copying is not permitted.

Use the graph to answer problems 3 and 4.

SOCCER GOALS SCORED THIS SEASON

Bears	⚽ ⚽ ⚽ ⚽ ⚽
Cheetahs	⚽ ⚽
Eagles	⚽ ⚽ ⚽ ⚽ ⚽
Falcons	⚽ ⚽ ⚽ ⚽ ⚽ ⚽ ⚽
Lions	⚽ ⚽ ⚽
Tigers	⚽ ⚽ ⚽ ⚽ ⚽ ⚽ ⚽ ⚽

Each ⚽ stands for 2 goals.

3 Tell whether each sentence is *True* or *False*.

a. The Eagles scored 10 goals. ☐ True ☐ False

b. The Lions scored 3 goals. ☐ True ☐ False

c. The Tigers scored as many goals as the Bears and the Lions combined. ☐ True ☐ False

d. The Falcons scored two more goals than the Eagles. ☐ True ☐ False

4 Sally chooses teams that together scored 20 goals. What teams might Sally choose?

Show your work.

Answer _____

_____

✓ **Self Check** *Go back and see what you can check off on the Self Check on page 179.*

In Lesson 24, you learned to read pictographs and bar graphs with scales. Take a look at this problem.

Tess has a game with letter tiles. Each tile shows one of the letters A, C, S, or T. Tess wants to make a pictograph showing the number of tiles with each letter.

S	S	S	S	S	C	C	C	C	C	T	T	T	T	T
A	A	A	A	A	T	T	T	T	T	S	S	S	S	S
S	S	S	S	S	A	A	A	A	A	T	T	T	T	T
A	A	A	A	A	S	S	S	S	C	C	C	C	C	
S	S	S	S	S	A	A	A	A	A					

🔍 Explore It

Use the math you already know to think about the problem.

◾ How many tiles have the letter A? _____

◾ How many tiles have the letter C? _____

◾ How many tiles have the letter S?_____

◾ How many tiles have the letter T? _____

◾ How many tiles are there in all? _____

◾ Suppose Tess uses this key: Each ☐ stands for 1 letter tile.
   How many pictures will she have to draw on the pictograph? _____

◾ Explain how Tess could change the key so that she could draw fewer ☐ on her pictograph.

   _____

   _____

©Curriculum Associates, LLC   Copying is not permitted.

Find Out More

Graphs can help us see and understand lots of data at once. Tess wants to draw a pictograph to show the letters on 70 different tiles. That is a lot of data to show!

In her pictograph, Tess uses symbols to show the data. The key for her pictograph tells how many letter tiles each symbol stands for. A key that stands for more than 1 makes it easier to show lots of data.

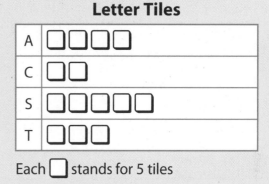

Letter Tiles

Each ☐ stands for 5 tiles

Tess uses the key: "Each ☐ stands for 5 tiles." 5 is a good choice for a key, because it is easy to show all of the data as groups of 5.

The same data can be shown on a bar graph. The bars show how many tiles there are for each letter. The numbers along the bottom of the bar graph are called the scale. The scale marks off equal sections. On this graph, the scale counts by 5s.

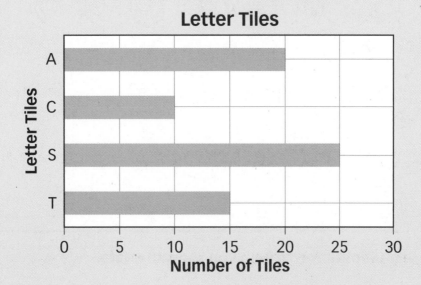

Reflect

1 Describe when you would use a scale greater than 1 for a pictograph or bar graph.

_____

_____

©Curriculum Associates, LLC   Copying is not permitted.

Read the problem below. Then explore different ways to show the data and make a pictograph.

Robert records the different bugs he sees. He wants to draw a pictograph using the data in the table. How can Robert make a pictograph?

Bugs Robert Saw

Type of Bug	Number of Bugs
ant	16
bee	4
moth	6
spider	12

Picture It

You can use models to show the data.

Use a scale of 2. Each ⬭ stands for 2 bugs.

Ant ⬭⬭⬭⬭⬭⬭⬭⬭

Bee ⬭⬭

Moth ⬭⬭⬭

Spider ⬭⬭⬭⬭⬭⬭

Model It

You can use multiplication to help you show the data.

Use a scale of 2. Each ◯ stands for 2 bugs.

To show 16 ants, use 8 ◯.	$16 = 8 \times 2$
To show 4 bees, use 2 ◯.	$4 = 2 \times 2$
To show 6 moths, use 3 ◯.	$6 = 3 \times 2$
To show 12 spiders, use 6 ◯.	$12 = 6 \times 2$

©Curriculum Associates, LLC   Copying is not permitted.

💡 Connect It

Now you will solve the problem from the previous page by drawing a graph.

2 What is a good title for Robert's graph? Write it on the graph.

Complete the key for the graph.

Use the data in the table and the key to complete the last two rows of the graph.

ant	Ⓐ	Ⓐ	Ⓐ	Ⓐ	Ⓐ	Ⓐ	Ⓐ	Ⓐ
bee	Ⓐ	Ⓐ						
_____								
_____								

Each Ⓐ stands for _____ bugs.

3 Why does a scale of 2 work better here than a scale of 1?

_____

_____

✏️ Try It

**Use what you just learned to solve this problem.
Show your work on a separate sheet of paper.**

4 Lin records the number of shells she collects at the beach.
Draw a pictograph of Lin's data. Use a scale of 10. Be sure
to write a title, a key, and draw the data.

Number of Shells Collected

Saturday	20 shells
Sunday	40 shells
Monday	30 shells
Tuesday	10 shells

Read the problem below. Then, explore different ways to show the data and make a bar graph.

Nan keeps track of how many minutes she practices the guitar each day. She wants to draw a bar graph using the data in the table. How can Nan make a bar graph?

Time I Practice Guitar	
Monday	5 minutes
Tuesday	30 minutes
Wednesday	15 minutes
Thursday	25 minutes
Friday	20 minutes

Picture It

You can use number lines to help you choose a scale.

The following number line has a scale of 5. The points on the number line show the number of minutes Nan practices each day.

Scale of 5

0   5   10   15   20   25   30   35   40

The following number line has a scale of 10. The points on the number line show the number of minutes Nan practices each day. Some points fall between the numbers on the scale.

Scale of 10

0   10   20   30   40

Model It

You can also use multiplication to help you know how to make a bar graph.

Multiply to find the numbers you would write on the bar graph scale. Use a scale of 5.

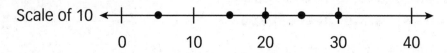

$1 \times 5 = 5$ $3 \times 5 = 15$ $5 \times 5 = 25$ $7 \times 5 = 35$

$2 \times 5 = 10$ $4 \times 5 = 20$ $6 \times 5 = 30$ $8 \times 5 = 40$

If you use a scale of 5, the scale numbers will be 5, 10, 15, 20, 25, 30, 35, 40.

©Curriculum Associates, LLC   Copying is not permitted.

Connect It

Now you will solve the problem from the previous page by drawing a graph.

5 How do you use the scale to help you draw the bars on a bar graph?

_____

6 What is a good title for Nan's graph?
   Write it on the graph.
   Write labels for the graph.
   Complete the scale.
   Draw the remaining bars on the graph.

7 Do you think a scale of 2 would work
   as well as a scale of 5 for this graph?
   Why or why not?

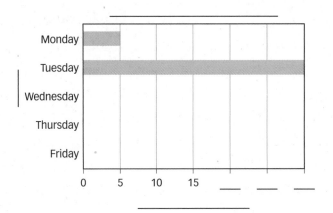

_____

_____

_____

Try It

Use what you just learned to solve this problem. Show your work on a separate sheet of paper.

8 The table shows how students get to school.

   Draw the bar graph on a separate sheet of paper. Be sure to write a title, choose a scale, label all the parts of the graph, and draw the bars.

Ways We Get to School

Way We Travel	Number
Bicycle	10
Bus	80
Car	40
Walk	20

Study the model below. Then solve problems 9–11.

Are the numbers in the data set multiples of 2 or multiples of 3?

Student Model

Sean asks his classmates to choose their favorite color bike. He recorded the results in this table. He wants to draw a bar graph of the data. How can he decide what scale to use?

Favorite Color Bikes

Color	Number
Blue	12
Green	6
Orange	3
Red	9

Look at how you could show your work using number lines.

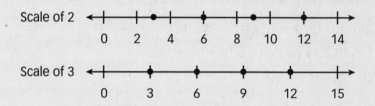

Scale of 2: 0 2 4 6 8 10 12 14

Scale of 3: 0 3 6 9 12 15

Solution: __Sean could look at the data and find a scale__

__that will be easy to use with the data. All the data are__

__multiples of 3, so 3 is a scale that makes sense.__

📝Pair/Share

How could you multiply to solve this problem?

Remember to write a title on your graph and label all the parts of your graph.

9 Draw a bar graph of the data in Sean's table.

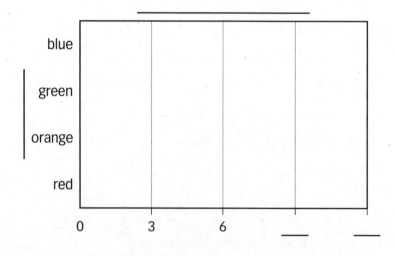

blue

green

orange

red

0   3   6   ___   ___

📝Pair/Share

Take a quick look at your graph. How can you tell that it is reasonable for the data you used?

©Curriculum Associates, LLC   Copying is not permitted.

10 Students recycled cans for the can drive. Elia recycled 20 cans. Liam recycled 40 cans. Jamal recycled 10 cans. Sara recycled 50 cans. Complete the pictograph of the recycling data.

Number of Cans Recycled

Elia	🛢	🛢			
Liam	🛢	🛢	🛢	🛢	

Each 🛢 stands for 10 cans.

The key on the graph is: Each 🛢 stands for 10 cans. How many cans should I draw next to Jamal's name?

Pair/Share

How can you use skip counting to check your answer?

11 Emilio begins to draw a pictograph of the data in the table.

Favorite Yogurt Flavor

Cherry	☺ ☺
Lemon	☺
Strawberry	☺ ☺ ☺ ☺
Vanilla	☺ ☺ ☺

Each ☺ stands for _____ students

Favorite Yogurt Flavor

Yogurt Flavor	Number of Students
Cherry	10
Lemon	5
Strawberry	20
Vanilla	15

I think I can compare the data in the table to the data in the graph to figure out the key.

Which key does Emilio use for his pictograph? Circle the letter of the correct answer.

A Each ☺ stands for 1 student.

B Each ☺ stands for 2 students.

C Each ☺ stands for 5 students

D Each ☺ stands for 10 students.

Vicky chose **C** as the correct answer. How did she get the answer?

_____

_____

Pair/Share

How can you check that Vicky's choice is correct?

Solve the problems.

Jane makes a bar graph of the number of tickets to the school play she sells each day.

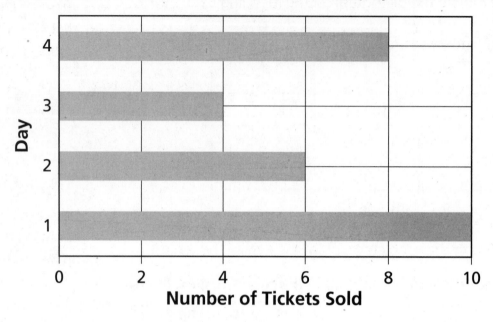

1   Tell whether each sentence is *True* or *False*.

   a. The scale for number of tickets sold in Jane's
       bar graph counts by 2.   ☐ True   ☐ False

   b. A good title for Jane's bar graph would be
       "Tickets Sold for Ten Days."   ☐ True   ☐ False

   c. If Jane had used a scale of 3 for her bar graph,
       she would have written the numbers 3, 6, 9, and
       12 on the scale.   ☐ True   ☐ False

   d. If Jane had used a scale of 3 for her bar graph,
       all of the bars would have ended between
       the numbers on the scale.   ☐ True   ☐ False

2   Suppose Jane made a pictograph of her data and used a ticket symbol to represent
   two tickets sold. How many ticket symbols would she need to show the number of
   tickets sold on Day 1?

   _____ symbols

©Curriculum Associates, LLC   Copying is not permitted.

3 Which set of data does Jane use to make the bar graph?

TICKETS SOLD

Day	1	2	3	4
Tickets Sold	4	2	3	5

A

TICKETS SOLD

Day	1	2	3	4
Tickets Sold	10	6	4	8

C

TICKETS SOLD

Day	1	2	3	4
Tickets Sold	4	8	6	10

B

TICKETS SOLD

Day	1	2	3	4
Tickets Sold	8	4	10	6

D

4 The table shows students' favorite games. Choose a scale for the data. Then use your scale to label and draw a pictograph of the data.

FAVORITE GAMES

Game	Number
Hopscotch	20
Jump Rope	10
Kick Ball	50
Tag	30

Each ☺ stands for _____ students

✓ **Self Check** *Go back and see what you can check off on the Self Check on page 179.*

Lesson 26   Part 1: Introduction
Measure Length and Plot Data on Line Plots

In Lesson 25, you drew pictographs and bar graphs. Now you will measure objects and draw line plots. Take a look at this problem.

Rosa is following directions for putting charms on a bracelet. She places her bracelet along the ruler. Draw a picture to show what Rosa's bracelet will look like when she is done.

Directions

Step 1: Place a ♥ at 1 inch.

Step 2: Place a ■ at $2\frac{1}{2}$ inches.

Step 3: Place a ♦ at $\frac{1}{4}$ inch.

Step 4: Place a ● at $1\frac{3}{4}$ inch.

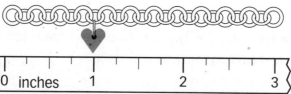

🔍 Explore It

Use the math your already know to solve this problem.

- Where should Rosa place the ♥ on the bracelet? at _____ inch

- Where should Rosa place the ■ on the bracelet? at _____ inches

- On a number line, $2\frac{1}{2}$ is between the numbers 2 and _____ .

- Rosa should place the ■ on the bracelet between 2 inches and _____ inches.

- Where should Rosa place the ♦ on the bracelet? at _____ inch

- On a number line, $\frac{1}{4}$ is between the numbers 0 and _____ .

- Rosa should place the ♦ on the bracelet between 0 inches and _____ inch.

- Explain how you could find where Rosa should place the ●.

_____

_____

©Curriculum Associates, LLC   Copying is not permitted.

🔍 Find Out More

Sometimes an object falls between the inch marks on a ruler, like in the bracelet problem. Then we measure to the nearest fraction of an inch. In this lesson, you will measure to the nearest half inch and to the nearest one-fourth inch.

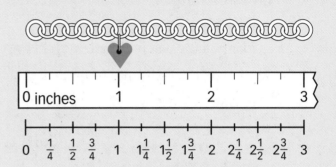

A ruler is like a number line. It shows whole numbers. It can also show fractions. This ruler shows half-inch marks and one-fourth-inch marks. Usually the fractions are not labeled on a ruler.

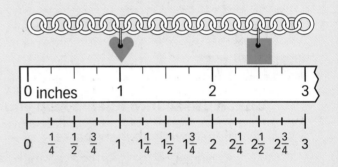

Rosa places the ■ at $2\frac{1}{2}$ inches. That is halfway between 2 inches and 3 inches on the ruler.

Rosa places the ◆ at $\frac{1}{4}$ inch. That is between 0 and 1 inch. It is closer to the 0 mark. She places the ● at $1\frac{3}{4}$ inches. That is between 1 inch and 2 inches. It is closer to 2 inches.

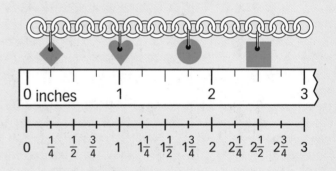

✏️ Reflect

1 Describe how to find the $1\frac{1}{2}$ inch mark on a ruler.

_____

_____

©Curriculum Associates, LLC   Copying is not permitted.

Read the problem below. Then explore different ways of showing how to measure length.

Brian is measuring the length of earthworms for his science project. He collects six worms. He wants to make a table of the length of the worms. What measurements will Brian write in his table?

Earthworm Lengths

Earthworm	A	B	C	D	E	F
Length (in inches)						

Picture It

You can use an inch ruler to help you understand how to measure length.

This ruler shows half-inch marks.
You can measure to the nearest $\frac{1}{2}$ inch.

This ruler shows one-fourth-inch marks.

You can measure to the nearest $\frac{1}{4}$ inch.

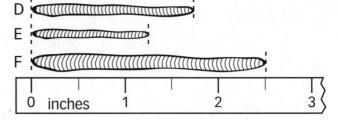

Model It

You can use words to describe how to measure length.

Line up the left end of the earthworm with zero on the ruler.

Look at the other end of the earthworm.

Find the mark on the ruler that is closest to the other end of the worm. You can measure to the nearest inch, $\frac{1}{2}$ inch, or $\frac{1}{4}$ inch.

©Curriculum Associates, LLC   Copying is not permitted.

Connect It

Now you will measure to solve the problem from the previous page.

Use what you just learned to solve these problems.

2 Complete the sentence to describe how you begin to measure earthworm A.

   I line up the left end of the earthworm with _____ on the ruler.

3 Is earthworm A longer than 1 inch or shorter than 1 inch? _____

4 The mark on the ruler that is closest to the other end of worm A is

   _____ inches.

5 Earthworm A is _____ inches long.

6 Measure earthworms B, C, D, E, and F. Write your measurements in the table.

Earthworm Lengths

Earthworm	A	B	C	D	E	F
Length (in inches)						

7 Explain how you found the length of earthworm F.

   _____

   _____

Try It

Use a ruler to measure each earthworm.

8 Brian finds two more worms. He labels them G and H. What are the lengths of the

worms to the nearest $\frac{1}{4}$ inch?

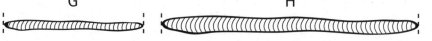

   Worm G is _____ inches long.   Worm H is _____ inches long.

Read the problem below. Then explore different ways to display the data.

Brian recorded the lengths of the earthworms in his table. He wants to make a line plot of the measurements. What will Brian's line plot look like?

Earthworm Lengths

Earthworm	A	B	C	D	E	F	G	H
Length (in inches)	$1\frac{1}{2}$	$2\frac{1}{2}$	2	$1\frac{3}{4}$	$1\frac{1}{4}$	$2\frac{1}{2}$	$1\frac{1}{2}$	$2\frac{3}{4}$

Model It

You can use a number line to help you begin to draw the line plot.

Earthworms are measured to the nearest $\frac{1}{4}$ inch.

The shortest earthworm is $1\frac{1}{4}$ inches

The longest earthworm is $2\frac{3}{4}$ inches

$$0 \quad \frac{1}{4} \quad \frac{1}{2} \quad \frac{3}{4} \quad 1 \quad 1\frac{1}{4} \quad 1\frac{1}{2} \quad 1\frac{3}{4} \quad 2 \quad 2\frac{1}{4} \quad 2\frac{1}{2} \quad 2\frac{3}{4} \quad 3$$

Model It

You can use models to help you display the data.

The following model shows the number of earthworms that are each length.

$1\frac{1}{4}$ inches	X
$1\frac{1}{2}$ inches	X X
$1\frac{3}{4}$ inches	X
2 inches	X
$2\frac{1}{4}$ inches	
$2\frac{1}{2}$ inches	X X
$2\frac{3}{4}$ inches	X

Each **X** stands for 1 earthworm.

©Curriculum Associates, LLC   Copying is not permitted.

Connect It

Now you will solve the problem from the previous page. Use the data in the table to help you complete the line plot.

Lengths of Earthworms Measured

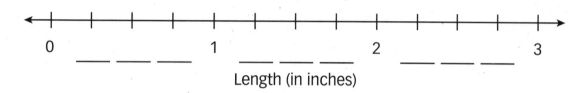

Length (in inches)

9 Complete the scale on the line plot number line. Use a scale of $\frac{1}{4}$ inch.

10 For each worm put an X on the line plot above the length of the worm. If there are two or more worms of the same length, put the Xs on top of each other. How many worms did Brian measure? _____

11 How many Xs will be on the line plot? _____

12 How many worms are $1\frac{1}{4}$ inches? _____ Draw that many Xs above $1\frac{1}{4}$.

13 How many worms are $1\frac{1}{2}$ inches? _____ Draw that many Xs above $1\frac{1}{2}$.

14 Complete the line plot. Draw an X for each earthworm measurement.

15 Explain what each X on the line plot stands for. _____

_____

Try It

Use what you just learned to solve this problem. Draw your line plot on a separate sheet of paper.

16 Draw a line plot of the data in the table.

Plant Lengths

Plant	A	B	C	D	E	F	G	H
Length (in inches)	$6\frac{1}{4}$	$6\frac{1}{2}$	$5\frac{3}{4}$	$6\frac{1}{2}$	$6\frac{3}{4}$	$6\frac{1}{4}$	$5\frac{3}{4}$	$6\frac{1}{2}$

The student lines up one end of the dragonfly wing with 0 on the ruler. Then the student finds the mark on the ruler closest to the other end of the wing.

Study the model below. Then solve problems 17–19.

Student Model

In science club, Lily measured the length of dragonfly wings. She made a line plot of her data. Then she found one more dragonfly wing.

Measure the wing to the nearest $\frac{1}{4}$ inch.

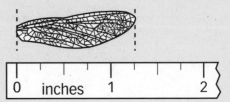

Show the measurement on Lily's line plot. Which wing length appears most often on the line plot?

Look at how you could show your work using a line plot.

Lengths of Dragonfly Wings Measured

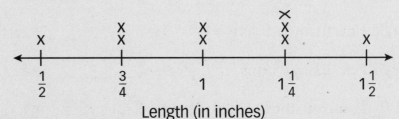

Length (in inches)

Solution: $1\frac{1}{4}$ inches

Pair/Share

How do you know which wing length appears most often?

17 How many dragonfly wings are shorter than 1 inch?

What does each X tell me?

Pair/Share

Describe how you found the answer.

Solution: _____

©Curriculum Associates, LLC   Copying is not permitted.

18 Lee measures the lengths of his friends' hands. He records the measurements in the table. Make a line plot of Lee's data.

Hand Lengths

Person	Arty	Leo	Meg	Olivia	Ruby	Zain
Length (in inches)	$5\frac{1}{2}$	5	$4\frac{3}{4}$	$5\frac{1}{2}$	5	$5\frac{3}{4}$

Lengths of Hands Measured

Length (in inches)

I can find the shortest measurement and the longest measurement to help me label the ends of my scale.

📱Pair/Share

Is there an X above every number on your line plot? Why or why not?

19 About how long is the marker to the nearest half inch? Circle the letter of the correct answer.

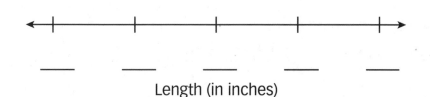

A 3 inches

B $3\frac{1}{4}$ inches

C $3\frac{1}{2}$ inches

D $4\frac{1}{2}$ inches

Vicky chose **B** as the correct answer. How did she get the answer?

_____

_____

_____

How can I find the nearest half inch on the ruler?

📱Pair/Share

Does Vicky's choice answer the question?

Solve the problems.

The line plot shows the lengths of toy planes. Use the line plot to answer problems 1–3.

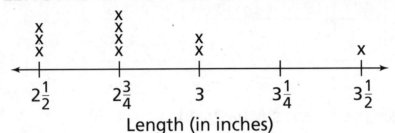

LENGTHS OF TOY AIRPLANES MEASURED

Length (in inches)

1 Which set of data was used to make the line plot?

A

TOY AIRPLANE LENGTHS (IN INCHES)

| $2\frac{1}{2}$ | $2\frac{3}{4}$ | 3 | $3\frac{1}{4}$ | $3\frac{1}{2}$ |

B

TOY AIRPLANE LENGTHS (IN INCHES)

| 3 | 4 | 2 | 0 | 1 |

C

TOY AIRPLANE LENGTHS (IN INCHES)

| $2\frac{1}{2}$ | $2\frac{1}{2}$ | $2\frac{1}{2}$ | $2\frac{3}{4}$ | $2\frac{3}{4}$ |
| $2\frac{3}{4}$ | $2\frac{3}{4}$ | 3 | 3 | $3\frac{1}{2}$ |

D

TOY AIRPLANE LENGTHS (IN INCHES)

| 3 | 4 | 2 | 0 | 1 |
| $2\frac{1}{2}$ | $2\frac{3}{4}$ | 3 | $3\frac{1}{4}$ | $3\frac{1}{2}$ |

2 Tell whether each sentence is *True* or *False*.

   a. There are four airplanes shown on the line plot. ☐ True ☐ False

   b. None of the airplanes measures $3\frac{1}{4}$ inches. ☐ True ☐ False

   c. All of the planes are longer than 2 inches. ☐ True ☐ False

   d. Exactly 3 planes measure $2\frac{3}{4}$ inches. ☐ True ☐ False

©Curriculum Associates, LLC   Copying is not permitted.

3   How long is the longest airplane measured? _____

4   Use an inch ruler for this problem.

Part A

Measure the leaves to the nearest one-fourth inch. Record the lengths in the table.

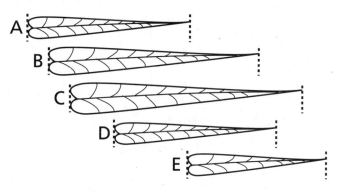

LEAF LENGTHS

Leaf	A	B	C	D	E
Length (in inches)					

Part B

Draw a line plot using the measurements you recorded in the table.

LENGTHS OF LEAVES MEASURED

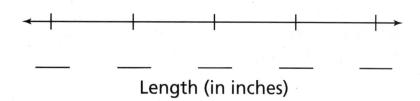

Length (in inches)

✓ **Self Check** *Go back and see what you can check off on the Self Check on page 179.*

Lesson 27   Part 1: Introduction 👥

Understand Area

CCSS
3.MD.C.5a
3.MD.C.5b
3.MD.C.6

What are some ways that we measure shapes?

Think about different ways you can measure a rug in the shape of a rectangle.

You can measure the length of the rug. The length tells how long the rug is from one end to the other. This rug is 3 feet long.

You can also measure the width of the rug. The width tells how wide the rug is from one side to the other. This rug is 2 feet wide.

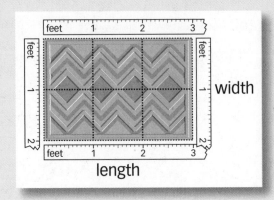

🔍 **Think**   When you measure area, you measure both length and width.

Suppose you have a string that is the same length as the rug. Can you use the string to cover the rug? No, the string is as long as the rug, but it is not as wide as the rug.

> **Underline the sentence that tells what area is.**

What if you stretched a string across the width of the rug? Could you use the string to cover the rug? No, the string is as wide as the rug, but it is not as long as the rug.

You want to find how much floor the rug covers, or the area of the rug.
Area is the amount of space a shape covers.

©Curriculum Associates, LLC   Copying is not permitted.

🔍 **Think** Area is the amount of space that a shape covers.

You measure area in **square units**.

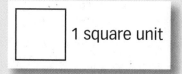
1 square unit

To measure area, you cover the shape with square units. All of the square units must be the same size.

Then you count to find how many square units cover the shape.

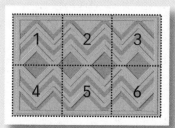

The area of the rug is 6 square units.

> *When I measure length, I make sure the zero mark on the ruler lines up with the edge of the shape. When I measure area, I make sure the square units line up with the edges of the shape.*

✏️ **Reflect**

1 Explain how you use square units to find the area of a shape.

_____

_____

_____

©Curriculum Associates, LLC   Copying is not permitted.

Explore It

You find area by measuring and counting square units.

Use an inch ruler to measure Square A.

2 Measure the length and width of one square unit in Square A.

The square unit is _____ inch long and _____ inch wide.

So, 1 square unit = _____ square inch.

3 Count the square inches in Square A to find the area.

The area of Square A is _____ square inches.

Use a centimeter ruler to measure Rectangle B.

4 Measure the length and width of one square unit in Rectangle B.

The square unit is _____ centimeter long and _____ centimeter wide.

So, 1 square unit =

_____ square centimeter.

5 Count the square centimeters in Square B to find the area.

The area of Square B is _____ square centimeters.

Square A

1 square unit

Rectangle B

1 square unit

Use both Square A and Rectangle B to answer these questions.

6 Can you use different-sized square units to find the area of a shape? _____

7 Does the size of the square unit change *how* you find area?

_____

_____

©Curriculum Associates, LLC   Copying is not permitted.

🗨 Talk About It

Solve the problems below as a group.

8 How is finding the area of the rectangle in square inches like finding the area in square centimeters? _____

_____

9 If you found the area of Square A in square centimeters, do you think the number of square centimeters in its area would be more or less than the number of square inches in its area? Explain. _____

_____

_____

10 Suppose you were measuring the area of a door. Would you need more square feet or more square inches to cover the door? Why? _____

_____

_____

11 Number each square unit in the shapes. Count to find the area.

   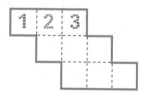

Area = _____ square units   Area = _____ square units

✏ Try It Another Way

Work with your group to find the area of each shape.

12

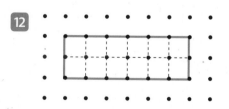

Area = _____ square units

13

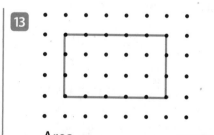

Area = _____ square units

Connect It

Talk through these problems as a class, then write your answers below.

14 Compare: Find the area of each shape.

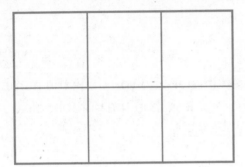

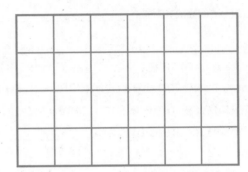

Each ☐ = 1 square unit   Each ☐ = 1 square centimeter

Area = _____   Area = _____

15 Examine: Anna counted the units in this rectangle. She said the area of the rectangle is 12 square units. What did Anna do wrong?

1	2	3
4	5	6
7	8	9
10	11	12

_____

_____

16 Relate: Think about how you could find the area of this shape.

First draw the square units.

Then number the square units to find the area of the shape.

Area = _____ square units

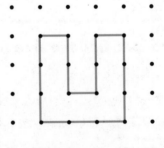

©Curriculum Associates, LLC   Copying is not permitted.

🔍 Put It Together

17 Use what you have learned to complete the task.

A Draw a rectangle with an area of 8 square centimeters.

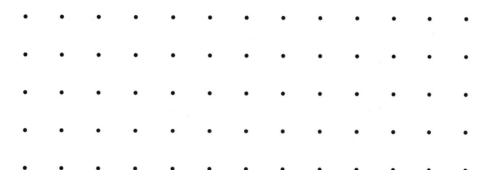

B Draw another rectangle with an area greater than 8 square centimeters.

C How did you know how to draw a rectangle with an area that is greater than 8 square centimeters?

_____

_____

_____

Lesson 28   Part 1: Introduction

Multiply to Find Area

CCSS
3.MD.C.7a
3.MD.C.7b

In Lesson 27, you learned to find the area of a rectangle by counting the number of square units that cover the rectangle. Take a look at this problem.

Some ink spilled on this rectangle. Jenny wants to find the area of the rectangle. How can she find the area without counting all of the square units?

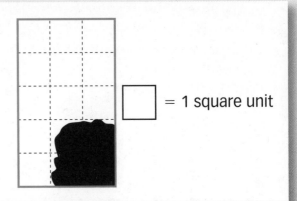

$\square$ = 1 square unit

🔍 Explore It

Use the math you already know to solve the problem.

● How many rows are in the rectangle? _____ rows
How many squares are in each row? _____ squares

● Multiply to find the number of squares that cover the rectangle.
5 rows of 3 squares ⟶ 5 × 3 = _____ squares

● How many columns are in the rectangle? _____ columns
How many squares are in each column? _____ squares

● Multiply to find the number of squares that cover the rectangle.
3 columns of 5 squares ⟶ 3 × 5 = _____ squares

● How many squares long is the rectangle? _____ squares
How many squares wide is the rectangle? _____ squares

● Explain how you could find the area using the length and the width of the rectangle. _____

_____

©Curriculum Associates, LLC   Copying is not permitted.

🔍 Find Out More

You can measure the area of a shape by counting the number of square units that cover it. Sometimes the squares units in rectangles are not shown, like in Jenny's rectangle. Other times, there are too many square units to count. There is another way to find the area of a rectangle.

You can multiply the number of rows by the number of columns to find the number of squares in the rectangle. There are 5 rows of squares in the rectangle. There are 3 columns of squares.

> 5 rows × 3 columns ⟶ 5 × 3 = 15, so there are 15 squares
>
> 3 columns × 5 rows ⟶ 3 × 5 = 15, so there are 15 squares

Now think about the length and the width of Jenny's rectangle.

5 units

3 units

> The rectangle is 5 squares long. Each square is 1 unit long.
> So the length is 5 units.
> The rectangle is 3 squares wide. Each square is 1 unit wide.
> So the width is 3 units.

You can multiply the length by the width to find the area. It is just like multiplying the number of rows by the number of columns in an array.

> 5 units × 3 units = 15 square units

The area of Jenny's rectangle is 15 square units.

✏️ Reflect

1 Where in real life have you seen rows of square tiles filling a rectangle?

_____

_____

Read the problem below. Then explore different ways to multiply to find area.

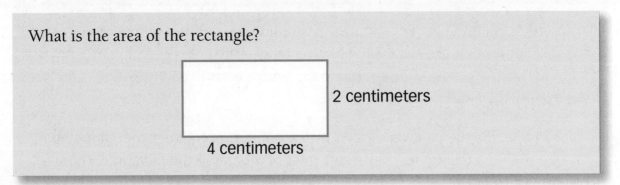

What is the area of the rectangle?

2 centimeters

4 centimeters

🔍 **Picture It**

You can use models to help you multiply to find area.

The following model shows the rectangle covered by square centimeters.

| 1 | 2 | 3 | 4 |
| 5 | 6 | 7 | 8 |

☐ = 1 square centimeter

🔍 **Model It**

You can also use a words to help you multiply to find area.

The rectangle is 4 centimeters long. The rectangle is 2 centimeters wide.

If I use 1-centimeter squares,
4 squares will fill a row.

If I use 1-centimeter squares,
2 squares will fill a column.

©Curriculum Associates, LLC   Copying is not permitted.

Connect It

Now you will solve the problem from the previous page using multiplication.

2 How many centimeters fit along the length of the rectangle? _____

What is the length of the rectangle? _____ centimeters

3 How many centimeters fit along the width of the rectangle? _____

What is the width of the rectangle? _____ centimeters

4 What does the problem ask you to find? _____

5 What unit is used to measure the area of this rectangle? _____

6 Write a number sentence to find the area of the rectangle.

length	×	width	=	area
_____ centimeters	×	_____ centimeters	=	_____ square centimeters

7 The area of the rectangle is _____ square centimeters.

8 Explain how you multiply to find the area of a rectangle. _____

_____

Try It

Use what you just learned about multiplying to find area to solve these problems. Show your work on a separate sheet of paper.

9 What is the area of this square?

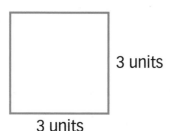
3 units

3 units

_____

10 A rectangle has a length of 6 inches and a width of 8 inches.

What is the area of the rectangle?

_____

©Curriculum Associates, LLC   Copying is not permitted.

Read the problem below. Then explore different ways to multiply to find area in a word problem.

Tyler's bedroom is 9 feet wide and 9 feet long. Suki's bedroom is 8 feet wide and 10 feet long. Who has the bedroom with the greater area?

Picture It

You can use models to help you multiply to find area.

The following models show the length and width of Tyler's and Suki's bedrooms.

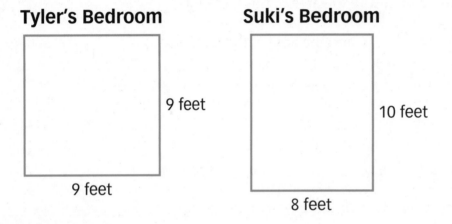

Tyler's Bedroom

9 feet

9 feet

Suki's Bedroom

10 feet

8 feet

Model It

You can also use words to help you multiply to find area.

Use words to describe each bedroom rectangle.

Tyler's room:

The length of the room is 9 feet.

The width of the room is 9 feet.

Suki's room:

The length of the room is 10 feet.

The width of the room is 8 feet.

©Curriculum Associates, LLC Copying is not permitted.

🔍 Connect It

Now you will solve the problem from the previous page using multiplication.

11 What does the problem ask you to find? _____

12 What units are used to measure the length and width of the bedrooms? _____

13 What unit do you use to record the area of the bedrooms? _____

14 Find the area of Tyler's bedroom.

length	×	width	=	area
_____ feet	×	_____ feet	=	_____ square feet

The area of the Tyler's bedroom is _____ square feet.

15 Find the area of Suki's bedroom.

length	×	width	=	area
_____ feet	×	_____ feet	=	_____ square feet

The area of the Suki's bedroom is _____ square feet.

16 So, _____ has the bedroom with the greater area.

17 Explain how you know that the area of Tyler's bedroom must have the label *square feet*. _____

_____

✏️ Try It

Use what you just learned about multiplying to find area to solve this problem.

18 Fran found the area of a rectangle by multiplying 5 units × 4 units. Draw Fran's rectangle. Label the side lengths. Write the area of the rectangle.

The student multiplies the length by the width to find the area. That's like multiplying the number of columns by the number of rows.

Pair/Share

How else could you solve this problem?

Study the model below. Then solve problems 19–21.

Student Model

Ms. Cruz is putting a carpet in the living room. How many square feet of carpet does Ms. Cruz need to cover the floor?

Living Room

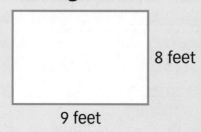

8 feet

9 feet

Look at how you could show your work using multiplication.

length	×	width	=	area
__9__ feet	×	__8__ feet	=	__72__ square feet

Solution: __72 square feet__

The sides of a square are all the same length.

19 Marcia finds the area of a square. The length of a side of the square is 5 centimeters. What is the area of the square?

Show your work.

Pair/Share

How did you and your partner solve this problem?

Solution: _____

©Curriculum Associates, LLC   Copying is not permitted.

20 Ms. Clark is building a patio that is 4 yards long and 3 yards wide. She has enough bricks to cover an area of 14 square yards. Does Ms. Clark have enough bricks to build the patio?

Show your work.

I think there are at least two different steps to solve this problem.

Solution: _____

_____

🗨 **Pair/Share**

How could you use a picture to solve this problem?

21 What is the area of the rectangle shown below? Circle the letter of the correct answer.

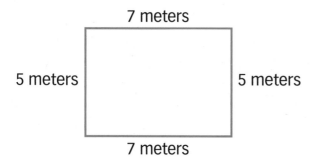

7 meters

5 meters   5 meters

7 meters

A   35 square meters

B   24 square meters

C   12 square meters

D   7 square meters

Bobby chose **B** as the correct answer. How did he get the answer?

_____

_____

To find the area of the rectangle, should you add or multiply?

🗨 **Pair/Share**

Do you need each side of the rectangle labeled with the length to solve the problem? Why or why not?

Solve the problems.

1 Mr. Frank is putting tile on the bathroom wall. How many square feet of tile does he need to buy?

A 49 square feet

B 42 square feet

C 26 square feet

D 13 square feet

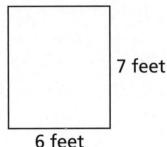

7 feet

6 feet

2 Which shape has an area of 12 square feet?

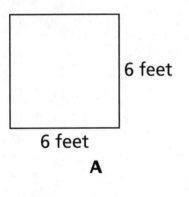

6 feet

6 feet

A

3 feet

3 feet

B

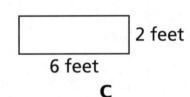

2 feet

6 feet

C

2 feet

4 feet

D

3 The area of a driveway is 24 yards. Choose **all** the possible dimensions of the driveway.

A Width: 4 yards Length: 8 yards

B Width: 6 yards Length: 4 yards

C Width: 6 yards Length: 3 yards

D Width: 4 yards Length: 6 yards

E Width: 3 yards Length: 8 yards

©Curriculum Associates, LLC   Copying is not permitted.

4 Rita is making a quilt. It is made with 45 square blocks of fabric and is 9 blocks long.

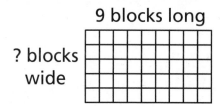

9 blocks long

? blocks wide

Use the numbers shown to fill in the blanks of the number sentence that can be used to find how many blocks wide the quilt is.

| 4 | 5 | 6 | 9 | 45 |

☐ × ☐ = ☐

5 Kayla draws this rectangle.

2 units

12 units

Part A

What is the area of Kayla's rectangle?

Answer _____ square units

Part B

James draws a rectangle with the same area but different length and width. What is a possible length and width for James' rectangle?

Answer _____

_____

 **Self Check** *Go back and see what you can check off on the Self Check on page 179.*

©Curriculum Associates, LLC   Copying is not permitted.

Lesson 29 Part 1: Introduction
Add Areas

CCSS

3.MD.C.7c
3.MD.C.7d

In Lesson 28, you learned how to count squares and use multiplication to find the areas of rectangles with whole-number sides. Now look at this problem.

Ana bought a movie poster that measured 3 feet long by 2 feet wide. Raul bought a movie poster that was 3 feet long by 1 foot wide. They plan to hang them on their classroom wall, as shown at the right.

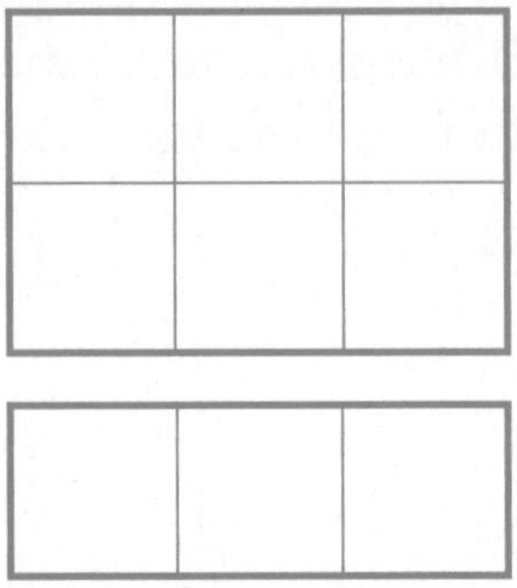

What is the total area of the wall that the movie posters will cover?

🔍 Explore It

Use the math you already know to solve the problem.

- How many squares cover Ana's movie poster? _____

- What is the measure of each square? _____

- What is the area of Ana's movie poster? _____

- 3 squares cover Raul's movie poster. What is the area of his poster?

  _____

- Explain how you can find the area of the wall that will be covered by both movie posters.

  _____

  _____

  _____

  _____

©Curriculum Associates, LLC   Copying is not permitted.

🔍 Find Out More

Remember that area is the number of square units that cover a shape. Sometimes, shapes are put together.

Think about the movie posters from the problem on the last page. Both movie posters are placed on the same wall. To find the total area of the posters, you can think of them as one large poster and multiply side lengths.

Or, you can multiply to find the area of each poster, then add those areas together.

1	2	3
4	5	6

7	8	9

1	2	3
4	5	6

6 square feet

7	8	9

3 square feet

6 square feet + 3 square feet = 9 square feet

✏️ Reflect

1 Describe how you can find the area of the shape shown below.

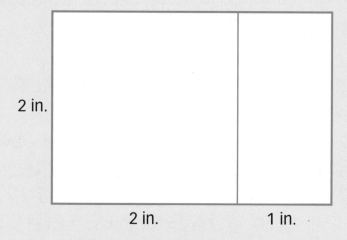

_____

_____

©Curriculum Associates, LLC   Copying is not permitted.

Read the problem below. Then explore different ways to find area.

This is Mrs. Chang's vegetable garden. The part on the left is for tomatoes. The part on the right is for corn.

What is the area of the garden?

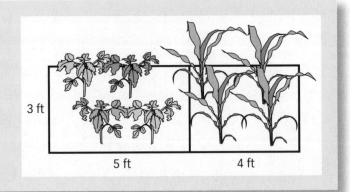

3 ft

5 ft   4 ft

🔍 Picture It

You can find the area of a shape by counting the number of square units that cover it.

1	2	3	4	5	6	7	8	9
10	11	12	13	14	15	16	17	18
19	20	21	22	23	24	25	26	27

There are 27 square units. Each square unit is 1 square foot.

🔍 Model It

You can find the area of a rectangle by multiplying the length by the width.

The width of the rectangle is 3 feet.

The length of the rectangle is equal to 5 feet + 4 feet, or 9 feet.

$3 \times 9 = 27$

The area is 27 square feet.

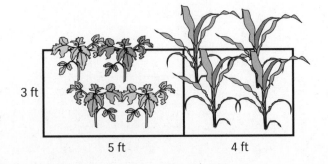

3 ft

5 ft   4 ft

©Curriculum Associates, LLC   Copying is not permitted.

Connect It

Now you will solve the problem from the previous page by breaking apart a number to make one hard multiplication sentence into two easier sentences.

2 Look at the Model It section on the last page. The equation $3 \times 9 = 27$ is used to find the area. Explain what each factor stands for in the multiplication sentence.

_____

3 The picture in the Model It section shows you a way to break apart the length into two smaller numbers. What are these two numbers? _____

4 You can use these numbers to find the areas of the parts of the garden.

$3 \times$ _____ = _____ $3 \times$ _____ = _____

5 You can add the areas of the garden parts to find the area of the whole garden.

_____ + _____ = 27

6 Explain how you can break apart the width of a rectangle into two smaller numbers to help you find its area. _____

_____

_____

Try It

Use what you just learned to solve these problems. Show your work on a separate sheet of paper.

7 What is the area of this figure?

_____

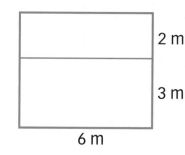

2 m

3 m

6 m

8 Mr. Davis wants to tile his closet and laundry room with 1 square foot tiles.

How many square foot tiles will Mr. Davis need?

_____

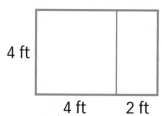

4 ft

4 ft   2 ft

Read the problem below. Then explore different ways to find areas of shapes.

Eden used square inch tiles to build the shape shown at the right.

What is the total area of Eden's shape?

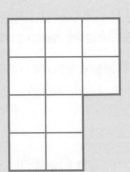

You can find the area of a shape by counting the number of square units that cover the shape.

There are 10 square units. Each square unit is 1 square inch.

1	2	3
4	5	6
7	8	
9	10	

You can find the area of a shape by breaking it apart into smaller shapes.

You can break apart Eden's shape into two smaller shapes like this:

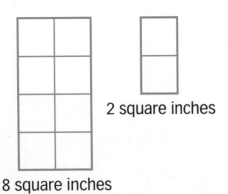

2 square inches

8 square inches

You can break apart Eden's shape into two different smaller shapes like this:

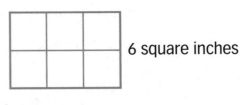

6 square inches

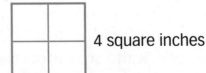

4 square inches

©Curriculum Associates, LLC   Copying is not permitted.

Connect It

Solve the problem from the previous page using multiplication and addition.

9 The Model It section shows two ways to break apart Eden's shape. Look at the first way. For each of the smaller shapes, write a multiplication sentence to show its area.

_____ × _____ = _____   _____ × _____ = _____

Write an addition sentence to show
the total area of Eden's shape.   _____ + _____ = _____

10 Look at the second way to break apart Eden's shape. For each of the smaller shapes, write a multiplication sentence to show its area.

_____ × _____ = _____   _____ × _____ = _____

Write an addition sentence to show
the total area of Eden's shape.   _____ + _____ = _____

11 Mike and Rick start with the same shape. Mike breaks apart the shape into two smaller shapes. Rick breaks apart the shape into two different smaller shapes. Is the total area of Mike's two shapes the same as the total area of Rick's two shapes? Explain how you know. _____

_____

_____

Try It

Use what you just learned about adding areas to solve these problems. Show your work on a separate sheet of paper.

12 This is Bethany's garage. What is the total area of Bethany's garage?

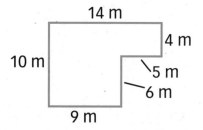

13 What is the area of this shape?

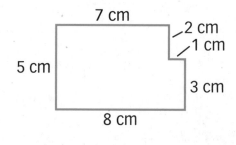

_____

Study the model below. Then solve problems 14–16.

Miguel broke apart the shape into 3 smaller rectangles and then added to find the total area.

Student Model

Miguel drew this shape in his notebook.

What is the total area of Miguel's shape?

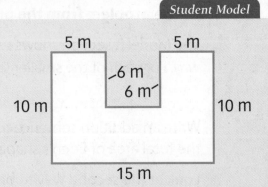

Look at how you could show your work by breaking apart the shape into three rectangles.

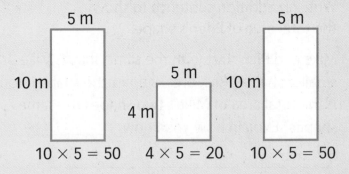

$10 \times 5 = 50$ $4 \times 5 = 20$ $10 \times 5 = 50$

Solution: __120 square meters__

📢Pair/Share

How else could the figure be broken apart?

I think there are at least two different ways I could solve this problem.

📢Pair/Share

Did you and your partner use the same method to solve? If not, discuss your methods.

14 What is the area of the shape below?

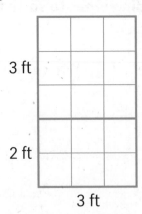

Solution: _____

©Curriculum Associates, LLC   Copying is not permitted.

15 Seth used 1-inch square tiles to build the shape shown below.

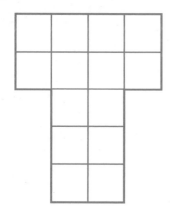

What is the total area of Seth's shape?

Solution: _____

How can counting help you solve this problem?

Pair/Share
How else could you solve this problem?

16 Kale drew a picture of a birdhouse.

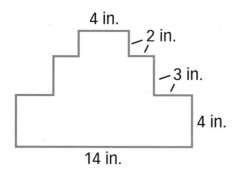

4 in.

2 in.

3 in.

4 in.

14 in.

What is the total area of the birdhouse? Circle the letter of the correct answer.

A 46 inches

C 88 inches

B 46 square inches

D 88 square inches

Sue chose **C** as the correct answer. How did she get that answer?

_____

_____

To find area, is it the distance around the figure or the number of square tiles that it covers?

Pair/Share
Does Sue's answer make sense?

©Curriculum Associates, LLC   Copying is not permitted.

Solve the problems.

1 Mrs. Ambrose drew this picture of her new patio and kitchenette.

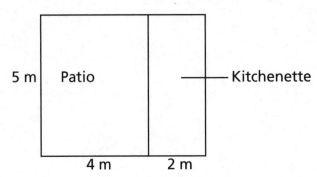

What is the total area of Mrs. Ambrose's new patio and kitchenette?

A 22 meters

C 30 meters

B 22 square meters

D 30 square meters

2 Below are two rectangles that are joined together.

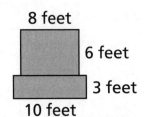

For numbers 2a–2d, choose *Yes* or *No* to indicate whether joining each rectangle to the existing two rectangles would total exactly 98 square feet.

a.
8 feet
3 feet

☐ Yes   ☐ No

b.
10 feet
2 feet

☐ Yes   ☐ No

c.
5 feet
4 feet

☐ Yes   ☐ No

d.
9 feet
2 feet

☐ Yes   ☐ No

©Curriculum Associates, LLC   Copying is not permitted.

3　Label the missing dimensions. Then divide the figure into two rectangles to find its area.

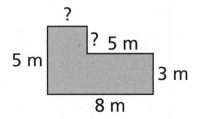

Answer　Area = _____ square meters.

4　Opal drew this picture of a picnic table.

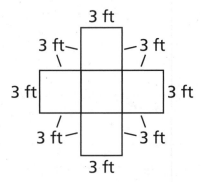

What is the total area of the picnic table? Break apart the picture into smaller rectangles, then use multiplication and addition to find the total area.

Show your work.

Answer　The total area of the picnic table is _____ square feet.

✓ **Self Check**　*Go back and see what you can check off on the Self Check on page 179.*

273
©Curriculum Associates, LLC　Copying is not permitted.

Lesson 30   Part 1: Introduction 👥

Connect Area and Perimeter

In Lessons 27–29, you have learned about finding the area of some shapes. Take a look at this problem.

Claire ran along the lines on the outside of the soccer field at school. She went around the whole field one time.

60 yards

40 yards   40 yards

60 yards

How far did Claire run?

🔍 Explore It

Use the math you already know to solve the problem.

● How many sides are there in all? _____

● How long are the long sides? _____

● How long are the short sides? _____

● Explain how you could use these numbers to figure out how far Claire ran.

_____

_____

©Curriculum Associates, LLC   Copying is not permitted.

Find Out More

You have already learned about finding the area of shapes. Area tells how much space a shape covers. The shaded part of the soccer field shows the area of the field.

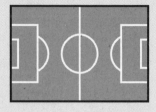

Perimeter tells you the total distance around a shape. The red line around the soccer field shows the perimeter of the field.

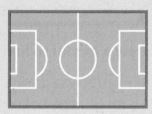

You can find the perimeter of a shape by adding the lengths of all the sides.

60 + 40 + 60 + 40 = 200

The perimeter of the soccer field is 200 yards.

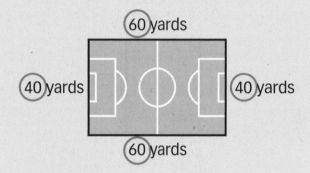

Reflect

1 Richard wants to put up a fence around his backyard. Does he need to find the area or the perimeter? What measurements does he need to find to figure out how much fence he needs? _____

_____

_____

©Curriculum Associates, LLC   Copying is not permitted.

Read the problem below. Then explore different ways to find the missing side length when you know the perimeter.

> Willis made an L-shaped pen for his pet rabbit. The pen has 6 sides, and the perimeter is 10 meters. The lengths of five of the sides are 1 meter, 3 meters, 2 meters, 1 meter, and 1 meter. What is the length of the sixth side?

🔍 Picture It

You can draw a model to help understand the problem.

An L-shaped figure was drawn to show the shape of the rabbit pen. The side lengths you were given have been labeled.

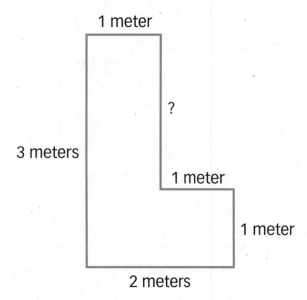

The perimeter of the pen is 10 meters. A ? is used to show to the side length you do not know.

©Curriculum Associates, LLC   Copying is not permitted.

Connect It

Now you will solve the problem from the previous page using an equation.

2 Explain how you would find the perimeter of the shape if you knew all of the side lengths. _____

_____

3 You know the perimeter is 10. Explain how you could figure out the side length that is missing. _____

_____

4 Write an equation to find the missing side length. Use a ? for the number you do not know. _____

5 What is the missing side length? _____

6 Explain how an addition equation can help you find the perimeter of a shape.

_____

_____

Try It

Use what you just learned about perimeter to solve these problems.

7 Jordan has a kite with four sides. Two of the sides are 8 inches long. Two of the sides are 12 inches long. What is the perimeter of the kite? _____

8 The perimeter of the shape below is 18 feet. What is the missing side length?

_____

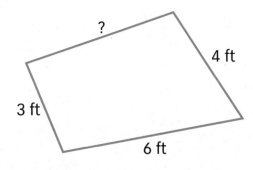

Read the problem below. Then explore different ways to find rectangles with the same area and different perimeters.

Emma drew this rectangle. What other rectangles have the same area?

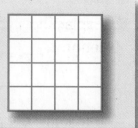

Picture It

You can use models to help you find rectangles with the same area and different perimeters.

The area of Emma's rectangle is 16 square units. The models below are two other rectangles. Each of these rectangles also has an area of 16 square units.

You can turn the first of these rectangles on its side to make a rectangle 1 unit long and 16 units wide. You can turn the second rectangle on its side to make a rectangle 2 units long and 8 units wide.

Model It

You can use a table to help you find rectangles with the same area and different perimeters.

You can make a table showing the different rectangles that have an area of 16 square units. The rectangle Emma drew is highlighted in red.

Length	Width	Area	Perimeter
16 units	1 units	16 square units	34 units
8 units	2 units	16 square units	20 units
4 units	4 units	16 square units	16 units
2 units	8 units	16 square units	20 units
1 units	16 units	16 square units	34 units

©Curriculum Associates, LLC   Copying is not permitted.

Connect It

Now think about how the problem was solved on the previous page.

9 How can you tell that the other rectangles pictured have the same area as Emma's?

_____

_____

10 To find other rectangles with an area of 16 square units, think of multiplication facts with a product of 16. What are the multiplication facts that have a product of 16? _____

How did Emma use those multiplication facts in the table from the Model It section? _____

_____

11 Can two rectangles have the same area but have different perimeters? How do you know? _____

_____

_____

Try It

Use what you just learned about area and perimeter to solve these problems.

12 Look at the rectangle below. Then draw another rectangle with the same area but different side lengths.

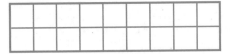

13 Look at the rectangle you drew in problem 12. Is its perimeter the same, greater than, or less than the first rectangle's perimeter? _____

©Curriculum Associates, LLC   Copying is not permitted.

Read the problem below. Then explore different ways to find rectangles with the same perimeter and different areas.

> Kai drew the rectangle below. What other rectangles have the same perimeter?

 **Picture It**

You can use models to help you find rectangles with the same perimeter and different areas.

The perimeter of Kai's rectangle is 12 units. The models below show four other rectangles with a perimeter of 12 units.

Model It

You can use a table to help you find rectangles with the same perimeter and different areas.

You can make a table showing the different rectangles that have a perimeter of 12 units. The rectangle Kai drew is highlighted in red.

Length	Width	Area	Perimeter
1 unit	5 units	5 square units	12 units
2 units	4 units	8 square units	12 units
3 units	3 units	9 square units	12 units
4 units	2 units	8 square units	12 units
5 units	1 units	5 square units	12 units

©Curriculum Associates, LLC   Copying is not permitted.

Connect It

Now think about how the problem was solved on the previous page.

14 Look at the table. What do you notice about the sum of the length and the width of each rectangle? _____

How does the sum of the length and width compare to the perimeter?

_____

15 All of the rectangles have the same perimeter as Kai's rectangle. Only one has the same area as Kai's rectangle. What else is the same about that rectangle and Kai's rectangle? _____

_____

16 Can two rectangles have the same perimeter but have different areas? How do you know? _____

_____

_____

Try It

Use what you just learned about perimeter and area to solve these problems.

17 Look at the rectangle below. Then draw another rectangle with the same perimeter but different side lengths.

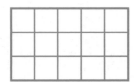

18 Look at the rectangle you drew in problem 17. Is its area the same, greater than, or less than the first rectangle's area? _____

Study the model below. Then solve problems 19–21.

Student Model

Look at the rectangle below. Then draw another rectangle with the same perimeter but a different area.

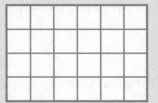

Look at how you could show your work using a drawing.

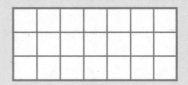

The perimeter of the rectangle is 20 units, and the area is 24 square units. The new rectangle needs to have a perimeter of 20 units, too.

💬 Pair/Share

What other rectangles would also be correct?

The sides of a square are all the same length. How many sides do you need to add together to find the perimeter?

💬 Pair/Share

What equation could you write to find the perimeter?

19 Jared's dad built a square deck in his backyard. One side of the deck is 10 feet long. What is the perimeter of the deck?

Show your work.

Solution: _____

©Curriculum Associates, LLC   Copying is not permitted.

20 Look at the rectangle below. Then draw another rectangle with the same area but a different perimeter.

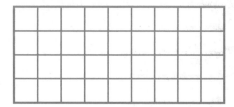

Show your work.

The area is 36 square units. What numbers, other than 4 and 9, are factors of 36?

Pair/Share

What other rectangle would have the same area and the same perimeter?

21 The perimeter of the shape below is 12 cm.

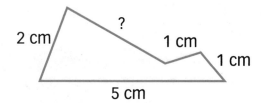

2 cm   ?   1 cm   1 cm   5 cm

What is the missing side length? Circle the letter of the correct answer.

A 2 cm

B 3 cm

C 4 cm

D 9 cm

Rose chose **D** as the correct answer. How did she get that answer?

_____

_____

You could write an equation with a ? for the missing number to show the perimeter.

Pair/Share

Does Rose's answer make sense?

Solve the problems.

1 Su drew a rectangle that is 6 inches long and 5 inches wide. What is the perimeter of the rectangle?

A 11 inches

C 22 inches

B 17 inches

D 30 inches

2 Rachel has 20 feet of fencing to section off a rectangular patch of her lawn. The fencing must go around the perimeter of the rectangular section with no overlap.

For numbers 2a–2d, select *Yes* or *No* to indicate whether Rachel has exactly enough fencing for each rectangular section shown.

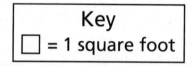

Key
☐ = 1 square foot

a. ☐ Yes ☐ No

b. ☐ Yes ☐ No

c. ☐ Yes ☐ No

d. ☐ Yes ☐ No

3 Which of the following is an example of perimeter? There may be more than one answer.

A grass covering a backyard

D the fence around a park

B the border around a picture

E the amount of water in a swimming pool

C carpet in a room

©Curriculum Associates, LLC Copying is not permitted.

4   Look at the rectangle below.

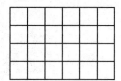

Part A

Find the perimeter and area of the rectangle.

Perimeter: _____   Area: _____

Part B

Use the grid to draw a rectangle that has the same perimeter but a different area than the original rectangle. Find the perimeter and area of your new rectangle.

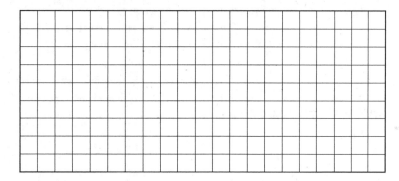

Perimeter: _____   Area: _____

Part C

Use the grid to draw a rectangle that has the same area but a different perimeter than the original rectangle. Find the perimeter and area of your new rectangle.

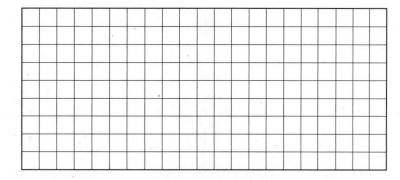

Perimeter: _____   Area: _____

✓ **Self Check**   *Go back and see what you can check off on the Self Check on page 179.*

©Curriculum Associates, LLC   Copying is not permitted.

Solve the problems.

1 The bar graph shows the number of diners who ate lunch at Bob's Diner each day for three days.

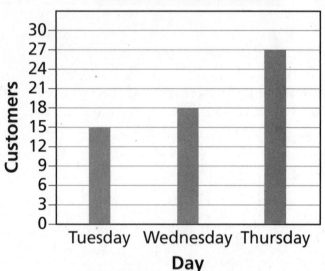

How many more people ate lunch at Bob's Diner on Thursday than on Tuesday?

A 12 people   **C** 27 people

B 15 people   **D** 30 people

2 Which of the following would you measure in kilograms? Circle the letter for all that apply.

A a person's weight

B the height of a tree

C the time it takes to drive to school

D the area of a garden

E the perimeter of a picture

3 Use the diagram shown. Which statements are true? Circle the letter for all that apply.

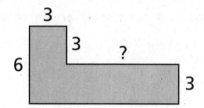

A If the missing side length is 8, the perimeter is 23.

B If the missing side length is 9, the perimeter is 36.

C If the missing side length is 8, the area is 42.

D If the missing side length is 9, the area is 45.

E If the missing side length is 10, the area is 39.

4 Angelica left home at 7:48. It took her 27 minutes to get to school. Draw hour and minute hands on the clock below to show what time she arrived at school.

©Curriculum Associates, LLC   Copying is not permitted.

5   Mark has 15 red balloons, 12 green balloons, 9 blue balloons, and 18 yellow balloons.

Part A

You are going to draw a pictograph of the data. Why might you want each picture to stand for more than 1 balloon?

_____

Part B

Draw a pictograph for the data given in the table.

6   The lengths of ten strings are 4, $4\frac{1}{4}$, $4\frac{1}{4}$, $4\frac{3}{4}$, $4\frac{1}{2}$, $4\frac{1}{4}$, $4\frac{1}{4}$, $4\frac{1}{2}$, $4\frac{3}{4}$, and 5 inches.

Part A

Use a line plot to show the lengths of the strings.

Part B

What is the length of the most strings?

Answer _____ inches

©Curriculum Associates, LLC   Copying is not permitted.

Performance Task

Answer the questions and show all your work on separate paper.

Dan is planning to build a square porch attached to the side of his house. After the porch is built, he would like to cover it with patio tiles. Each square tile is 1 foot long on each side. The model below shows the dimensions of the porch and the lawn where he plans to build. How many tiles will he need for this project?

✓ CHECKLIST

Did you . . .

☐ Use a formula?

☐ Draw a diagram?

☐ Check that your answer makes sense?

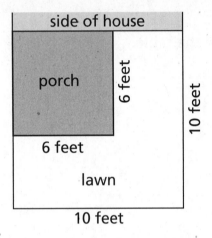

side of house

porch

6 feet

6 feet

10 feet

lawn

10 feet

After Dan bought all of the tiles, he changed his mind about the size of the porch. How could he change the dimensions of the porch, but still use the same number of tiles? Explain how you found your answer and draw a new plan for Dan's porch.

Reflect on Mathematical Practices

After you complete the task, choose one of the following questions to answer.

1. **Persevere** Is this problem mainly about area or perimeter? Explain how you know.

2. **Argue and Critique** How did you justify the dimensions you chose?

©Curriculum Associates, LLC   Copying is not permitted.

Unit 6
Geometry

Have you ever tried to describe the shape of something to a friend without being able to draw it? You might say, "It's sort of like a square." This doesn't give your friend many details about the shape. Does this mean that the shape has four sides? Are all of the sides equal in length? You might have said, "The shape has four sides and they are all equal in length." This still doesn't describe only one kind of shape.

In this unit, you will learn to recognize many four-sided figures and describe how they are alike and how they are different. You will also use what you know about area and fractions to split up shapes into equal parts.

✓ Self Check

Before starting this unit, check off the skills you know below. As you complete each lesson, see how many more you can check off!

I can:	Before this unit	After this unit
describe shapes, compare them, and put them in groups that tell how they are alike, for example: by the number of sides or if there are square corners.	☐	☐
compare quadrilaterals and put them in groups based on their attributes, for example: all four sides are equal or there are two pairs of parallel sides.	☐	☐
divide rectangles into equal parts and name the parts using fractions.	☐	☐

©Curriculum Associates, LLC   Copying is not permitted.

Lesson 31 Part 1: Introduction

Understand Properties of Shapes

CCSS
3.G.A.1

How do sides and angles help you to name shapes?

You can count the sides. This shape has 3 sides.

You can count the angles. This shape has 3 angles.

A shape with 3 sides and 3 angles is a triangle.

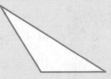

 Think   What are other ways to describe the sides of shapes?

Some shapes have sides with all different lengths.

Measure the sides of this shape. Use a centimeter ruler. Write the side lengths on the shape.

Some shapes have two or more sides that are the same length.

Sides A and B are the same length. Side C is a different length than sides A and B.

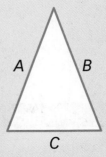

Shapes can have all sides the same length.

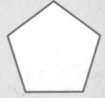

Shapes can have opposite sides that are the same length.

Sides A and C are the same length. Sides B and D are the same length.

©Curriculum Associates, LLC   Copying is not permitted.

🔍 **Think**　　What are other ways to describe the angles of shapes?

Shapes can have no square corners.

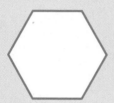

> *Angles that look like the corners of a square can be called square corners. Shapes that are not squares can have square corners, too.*

Shapes can have some square corners.

This triangle has 1 square corner.　　　　This **pentagon** has 2 square corners.

Shapes can have all square corners.

✏️ **Reflect**

1 What are some ways you can describe shapes?

_____

_____

_____

_____

🔍 Explore It

You can compare shapes and put them in groups. The groups tell how they are alike. Use these shapes to answer numbers 2 through 5.

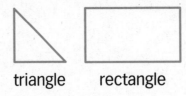

triangle   rectangle

2 Which of the shapes shown has at least one square corner?

_____

3 Which of the shapes shown has all square corners? _____

4 Which of the shapes shown has some sides that are the same length?

_____

5 Which of the shapes shown has opposite sides that are the same length?

_____

You can name shapes that belong to a group. You can also name shapes that don't belong to a group. Use these shapes to answer numbers 6 through 8.

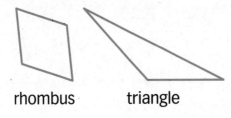

rhombus   triangle

6 Which of the shapes shown belongs to the group "all sides are the same length"?

_____

Which of the shapes shown does not belong to this group? _____

7 Which of the shapes shown belongs to the group "all sides are different lengths"?

_____

Which of the shapes shown does not belong to this group? _____

8 Name a different group that both the triangle and rhombus belong to.

_____

©Curriculum Associates, LLC   Copying is not permitted.

💬 Talk About It

Solve the problems below as a group.

9 Draw the two triangles on the previous page. Describe the sides and angles of each triangle in as many ways as you can.

_____   _____

_____   _____

_____   _____

10 Name two groups that both triangles belong to.

_____

✏️ Try It Another Way

Work with your group to fill in a Venn diagram.

11 A **Venn diagram** helps sort things into groups. Shapes that belong in different groups go in the left or right part. Shapes that belong in both groups go in the middle part. Draw a shape to match each description.

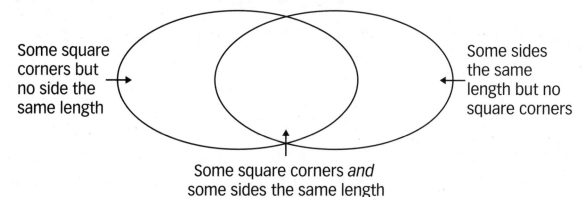

Some square corners but no side the same length

Some sides the same length but no square corners

Some square corners *and* some sides the same length

Connect It

Talk through these problems as a class, then write your answers below.

12 Compare: Think about how these shapes are alike and different. You can use a ruler to measure the sides.

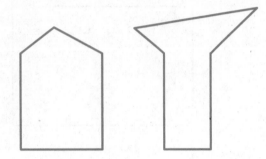

Write two ways in which these shapes are alike.

_____

_____

Write two ways in which these shapes are different.

_____

_____

13 Explain: Gwen says that all rectangles belong in the group "some square corners." Li says that all rectangles belong in the group "all square corners." Who is correct?

_____

_____

14 Illustrate: Draw a shape that belongs to both of these groups: "all sides are the same length" and "no square corners."

©Curriculum Associates, LLC   Copying is not permitted.

🔍 Put It Together

15 Use what you have learned to complete this task.

A Think about the ways you grouped shapes in this lesson. Think of two different ways you can put shapes into groups. Describe each group on the lines below.

Group 1: _____

Group 2: _____

Draw one shape that belongs to Group 1. Draw another shape that does not belong to Group 1.

       Belongs: Does not belong:

Explain why each shape does or does not belong to the group.

_____

_____

Draw one shape that belongs to Group 2. Draw another shape that does not belong to Group 2.

       Belongs: Does not belong:

Explain why each shape does or does not belong to the group.

_____

_____

B Is there a shape that belongs to both Group 1 and Group 2? Either draw a shape that belongs to both groups, or explain why there is no shape that belongs to both groups.

©Curriculum Associates, LLC   Copying is not permitted.

Lesson 32   Part 1: Introduction 👥

Classify Quadrilaterals

CCSS
3.G.A.1

In Lesson 31, you compared shapes and put them into groups. In this lesson, you will learn how to group quadrilaterals. Take a look at this problem.

A rhombus is one kind of quadrilateral. A rectangle is another kind of quadrilateral. How are a rhombus and rectangle the same? How are they different?

rhombus   rectangle

🔍 Explore It

Use the math you already know to solve the problem.

- Which shape or shapes have 4 sides and 4 angles? _____

- Which shape or shapes have 2 pairs of sides the same length?

    _____

- Which shape has 4 equal sides? _____

- Which shape has 4 square corners? _____

- How are a rhombus and rectangle alike? How are they different?

    _____

    _____

    _____

    _____

©Curriculum Associates, LLC   Copying is not permitted.

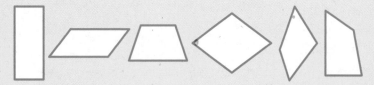 Find Out More

A **quadrilateral** is any shape with 4 sides and 4 angles.

You can name quadrilaterals using their attributes. An **attribute** is a way to describe a shape, like number of sides, or length of sides. One attribute is "4 sides." Another attribute is "at least 1 square corner."

Here are some ways you can name a quadrilateral:

It is a **parallelogram** if it has 2 pairs of **parallel** sides and 2 pairs of sides that are the same length. Parallel means always the same distance apart.

These are parallelograms:    These are not parallelograms:

It is a rectangle if it has 4 square corners. It also has 2 pairs of parallel sides and 2 pairs of sides that are the same length.

These are rectangles:    These are not rectangles:

It is a rhombus if it has 2 pairs of parallel sides and 4 sides that are all the same length.

These are rhombuses: These are not rhombuses:

Reflect

1 A square is a quadrilateral. Explain what a square is by writing about its sides and its corners.

_____

_____

Read the problem below. Then explore different ways to compare quadrilaterals.

Is a square a rectangle?

Is a rectangle a square?

 **Picture It**

You can use a drawing to compare quadrilaterals.

All quadrilaterals have 4 sides and 4 angles.

4 square corners
2 pairs of parallel sides
4 sides the same length

2 pairs of sides the same length
2 pairs of parallel sides
4 square corners

 **Model It**

You can use a table to compare quadrilaterals.

Shape	4 sides 4 angles	4 square corners	2 pairs of parallel sides	2 pairs of sides that are the same length	4 sides that are the same length
Square	✓	✓	✓	✓	✓
Rectangle	✓	✓	✓	✓	sometimes

©Curriculum Associates, LLC   Copying is not permitted.

Connect It

Now you will solve the problem from the previous page by comparing attributes.

2 What is an attribute of a square that is NOT an attribute of a rectangle?

_____

3 Does a rectangle have all the attributes of a square? _____

4 Does a square have all the attributes of a rectangle? _____

5 Is every square a rectangle? Explain why.

_____

_____

6 Is every rectangle a square? Explain why.

_____

_____

Try It

Use what you just learned about comparing quadrilaterals to solve these problems.

7 Circle all the quadrilaterals that are squares.

8 Circle all the quadrilaterals that are rectangles.

Read the problem below. Then explore different ways to name and draw quadrilaterals.

> I have a quadrilateral. It has 4 sides that are all the same length.
> It is not a square. What is the name of the shape?

 **Model It**

You can make a model to help name a quadrilateral.

Cut 4 strips of paper all the same length. Arrange them to look like a quadrilateral. It's not a square, so it can't have square corners.

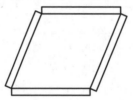

Solve It

You can make a list of the attributes to help you name a quadrilateral.

Look at the model above. Think about everything you know about this shape.

- It is a quadrilateral, so it has 4 sides and 4 angles.

- It has 4 sides that are all the same length.

- It is not a square, so it does not have square corners.

Using this list of attributes, you know that the shape is a rhombus.

©Curriculum Associates, LLC   Copying is not permitted.

🔍 Connect It

Now you will solve a problem like the one on the previous page.

This shape is on a food label.
Is it a quadrilateral?
Is it a parallelogram?
Is it a rectangle?
Is it a square?

9 How many sides and angles does the shape have? _____

10 Does the shape have parallel sides? _____

11 Does the shape have square corners? _____

12 Does the shape have 2 pairs of sides the same length? _____

13 Is the shape a quadrilateral? Explain why or why not.

_____

_____

14 Is the shape a parallelogram, a rectangle, or a square? Explain.

_____

_____

_____

✏️ Try It

Use what you just learned about naming and drawing quadrilaterals to solve these problems. Show your work on a separate piece of paper.

15 Circle all the quadrilaterals that have 2 pairs of sides the same length, but are NOT rectangles.

16 Draw a quadrilateral that has at least 1 square corner, but is NOT a rectangle.

©Curriculum Associates, LLC   Copying is not permitted.

Study the model below. Then solve problems 17–19.

The student used a geoboard to model the shape. Now you can see what the shape looks like.

Student Model

A patio has 2 pairs of parallel sides and 2 pairs of sides that are the same length. There are 4 square corners. What shape is the patio?

Look at how you could show your work using a model.

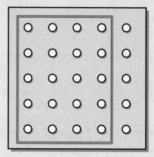

Solution: __The patio is a rectangle.__

💬**Pair/Share**

How else could you model the shape?

The shape you draw will not be a rectangle or a square. It will not be a parallelogram or a rhombus.

17 Draw a quadrilateral that has no sides the same length, no parallel sides, and no square corners.

Show your work.

💬**Pair/Share**

Can you draw a different shape that also solves the problem?

©Curriculum Associates, LLC   Copying is not permitted.

18 Friona cut along the dotted line on this piece of paper. She knows that she made two quadrilaterals.

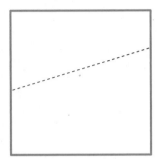

It may help to list the attributes of a parallelogram.

Is either of Friona's quadrilaterals a parallelogram? Explain why or why not.

Solution: _____

_____

💬**Pair/Share**

List the attributes of each of Friona's quadrilaterals.

19 Which shape is NOT a rectangle? Circle the letter of the correct answer.

A

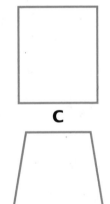

C

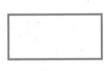

B

D

What are the attributes of each of the given shapes?

Ari chose **A** as the correct answer. How did he get that answer?

_____

_____

_____

💬**Pair/Share**

Why do you think Ari chose the answer that he did?

Solve the problems.

1 A rhombus must have all of these attributes except which one?

   A   4 sides that are the same length

   B   2 pairs of parallel sides

   C   4 square corners

   D   4 sides and 4 angles

2 Which of these can NOT be used to name this shape?

   A   quadrilateral   **C**   rhombus

   B   parallelogram   **D**   rectangle

3 Tell whether each sentence is *True* or *False*.

   a.   All rhombuses are quadrilaterals.   ☐ True   ☐ False

   b.   All rectangles are squares.   ☐ True   ☐ False

   c.   All parallelograms are rectangles.   ☐ True   ☐ False

   d.   All quadrilaterals are parallelograms.   ☐ True   ☐ False

   e.   All squares are rhombuses.   ☐ True   ☐ False

©Curriculum Associates, LLC   Copying is not permitted.

4   What is the *best* name that describes all the figures below? _____

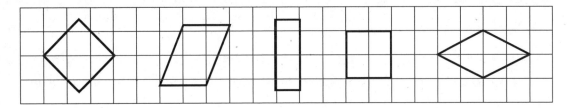

5   Draw a quadrilateral that belongs to at least two of these groups: parallelogram, rectangle, or square. Explain why your shape belongs to these groups.

Show your work.

Answer _____

6   Draw a quadrilateral that does not belong to any of these groups: parallelogram, rectangle, square. Explain why your shape does not belong to any of these groups.

Show your work.

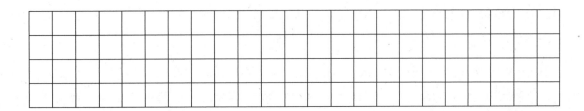

Answer _____

 **Self Check**   *Go back and see what you can check off on the Self Check on page 289.*

Lesson 33   Part 1: Introduction

Divide Shapes Into Parts With Equal Areas

You have learned about equal parts of shapes and finding area. In this lesson you will learn how to form and break apart rectangles into squares of equal area.

Students at Memorial School painted square tiles. The tiles were put together to make designs on the office walls. Each design is a rectangle made from 12 tiles. What are some different rectangles that can be made using the 12 tiles?

🔍 Explore It

Explore It

- ▪ What if you put the tiles in rows of 3? How many rows would you need to make a rectangle? _____ Draw squares in this rectangle to show what this looks like.

- ▪ Imagine you turned the rectangle on its side. Now how many rows does the rectangle have? _____ How many tiles are in each row? _____ Draw squares in this rectangle to show what this looks like.

- ▪ There are other ways to make rectangles with 12 squares. Explain how you would find the other ways. On a separate piece of paper, make drawings to show what the rectangles look like.

_____

_____

_____

©Curriculum Associates, LLC   Copying is not permitted.

🔍 Find Out More

On the previous page you made different rectangles using the same squares. You can also divide the same rectangle into parts that are different shapes and sizes.

 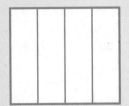  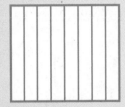

Equal parts of the rectangle cover an equal area. Think of these parts as fractions of the whole area. Each of the shaded parts shows $\frac{1}{4}$ of the area of the rectangle.

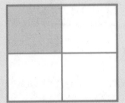 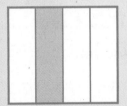 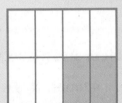 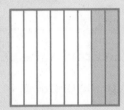

You can see that the shaded areas are in different parts of the rectangle. It doesn't matter where in the rectangle the shaded parts are. They still show $\frac{1}{4}$ of the area of the rectangle.

The first two rectangles show 1 of 4 equal parts shaded. The second two rectangles show 2 of 8 equal parts shaded. All shaded areas are equal in size even though the shapes and number of parts are different.

✏️ Reflect

1 If you divide a rectangle into 6 same-sized squares, are the areas of the squares equal? What do you know about the area of each square compared to the area of the whole rectangle?

_____

_____

©Curriculum Associates, LLC　Copying is not permitted.

Read the problem. Then explore different ways to divide rectangles.

Brett folded a piece of paper four times. His folds are shown below. Then he unfolded the paper. How many rows did Brett make? How many parts were in each row?

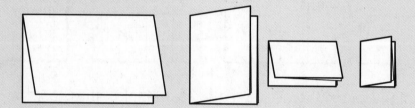

🔍 Model It

You can act out the problem and make a model.

Fold a piece of paper in half 4 times. This is what it looks like when you unfold it.

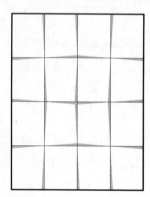

🔍 Solve It

You can use the model to solve the problem.

Count the rows. Count the rectangles in each row.

There are 4 rows of 4 rectangles.

Use multiplication to check that there are 16 parts in all.

$4 \times 4 = 16$

©Curriculum Associates, LLC   Copying is not permitted.

Connect It

Now you will solve the problem from the previous page.

The art teacher asked the students to color $\frac{1}{4}$ of the folded paper red. Brett colors 1 row of the paper. Did he color $\frac{1}{4}$ of the paper?

2 How many rows are on Brett's paper? _____

3 What fraction of the whole paper is 1 row? Explain.

_____

4 Did Bret color $\frac{1}{4}$ of the paper? _____

5 How else could Brett have colored $\frac{1}{4}$ of the paper?

_____

_____

6 To cover $\frac{1}{4}$ of the paper red, does Brett have to color 4 parts that are next to each other? Explain.

_____

_____

Try It

Use what you just learned about dividing rectangles to solve these problems. Show your work on a separate piece of paper. Use a ruler to help you.

7 Divide this rectangle into 8 equal squares. What fraction of the whole rectangle is each part? _____

8 Draw a picture of the rectangle from problem 7. Show a different way to divide it into 8 equal parts. What fraction of the whole rectangle is each part? _____

Study the model below. Then solve problems 9–11.

The student used a grid to make a model of the gameboard.

Student Model

A rectangular game board is divided into equal squares. There are 5 equal rows. Each row has 4 squares. Each row covers what fraction of the whole board?

Look at how you could show your work using a model.

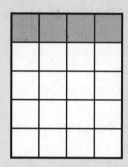

1 row out of 5 rows is $\frac{1}{5}$.

Solution: ___Each row covers $\frac{1}{5}$ of the whole gameboard.___

Pair/Share

How could you solve the problem without using a model?

9 Kevin has a rectangular garden. He wants to divide it into 12 equal sections. Show one way to do this. How many rows are there and how many sections are in each row?

Show your work. Use a ruler.

Can you use multiplication or division facts to help?

Solution: _____

Pair/Share

What is a different way to divide the garden into 12 equal sections?

©Curriculum Associates, LLC   Copying is not permitted.

10 Shade $\frac{1}{3}$ of this rectangle. How many equal squares does it take to cover $\frac{1}{3}$ of the rectangle?

Show your work.

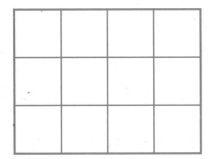

Solution: _____

11 A rectangle is divided into 2 rows of 6 equal squares. What fraction of the whole rectangle is each square? Circle the letter of the correct answer.

A $\frac{1}{2}$

B $\frac{1}{3}$

C $\frac{1}{6}$

D $\frac{1}{12}$

Ben chose **A** as the correct answer. How did he get that answer?

_____

_____

Remember that $\frac{1}{3}$ means 1 out of 3 equal parts.

Pair/Share

What fraction of the whole rectangle is 1 row?

How many squares are in the whole rectangle?

Pair/Share

What do you think Ben was thinking when he got this answer?

Solve the problems.

1 A rectangle is divided into 15 equal squares. How many squares make up $\frac{1}{3}$ of the rectangle?

A 3 squares   **C** 6 squares

B 5 squares   **D** 10 squares

2 A rectangle is divided into equal squares. One row covers $\frac{1}{8}$ of the whole rectangle. There are 3 squares in each row. How many squares are in the whole rectangle?

A 8 squares   **C** 24 squares

B 18 squares   **D** 32 squares

3 A teacher divides a rectangular bulletin board into equal parts. There is 1 part for each of 36 students. Choose either *Yes* or *No* to tell whether the plan described will do this.

a. Make 4 rows of 9 parts.   ☐ Yes   ☐ No

b. Make 6 rows of 6 parts.   ☐ Yes   ☐ No

c. Make 8 rows of 4 parts.   ☐ Yes   ☐ No

d. Make 3 rows of 12 parts.   ☐ Yes   ☐ No

e. Make 7 rows of 5 parts.   ☐ Yes   ☐ No

4 Shade $\frac{6}{8}$ of the rectangle below.

©Curriculum Associates, LLC   Copying is not permitted.

5 Mark is tiling a square floor. The model below shows how much of the job he has finished. How many tiles are needed to cover the whole floor?

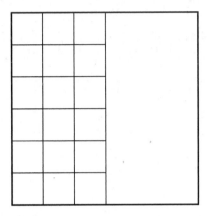

Show your work. Use a ruler.

Answer _____ tiles

6 The rectangles below are all the same. Dani wants to shade $\frac{1}{3}$ of each rectangle. Use the 3 rectangles below to show 3 different ways to shade $\frac{1}{3}$.

  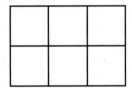

How many squares do you need to shade to cover $\frac{1}{3}$ of one of the rectangles?

Answer _____ squares

✓ **Self Check** *Go back and see what you can check off on the Self Check on page 289.*

Solve the problems.

1 Which figure has the most square corners?

A

B

C

D

2 Which quadrilateral has 4 sides that are the same length and 4 angles that are not square corners?

A

B

C

D

3 Choose **all** the terms that describe the shape below.

A quadrilateral

B parallelogram

C rectangle

D rhombus

E square

4 Which rectangles have $\frac{1}{3}$ shaded?

A

B

C

D

©Curriculum Associates, LLC   Copying is not permitted.

5 Sort the following four shapes according to the categories in the boxes below. Sketch the shape in each of the boxes where it belongs.

Has at least 1 square corner	Is a parallelogram	All sides are the same length

6

Part A

A rectangle is shown below. All of the sections are the same size.

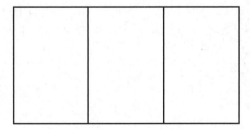

What fraction of the total figure is each section?

Answer _____

Part B

Use a ruler to draw a square and divide it into equal sections so that each section is $\frac{1}{8}$ of the area of the square.

Performance Task

Answer the questions and show all your work on separate paper.

Read each riddle below. Use the clues to draw the figure or figures you think they describe. Name the figures when possible. A riddle may have more than one correct answer.

✓ **CHECKLIST**

Did you . . .

☐ Use vocabulary from the unit?

☐ Use a ruler?

☐ Check your definitions?

1. "I'm a four sided figure. What could I be?"

2. "I'm a four sided figure. I have two sets of parallel sides. What could I be?"

3. "I'm a four sided figure. I have two sets of parallel sides. All of my sides are the same length. What could I be?"

4. "I'm a four sided figure. I have two sets of parallel sides. All of my sides are the same length. I have four square corners. What could I be?"

Choose two of these figures and write a riddle for each. Each riddle should have at least three clues.

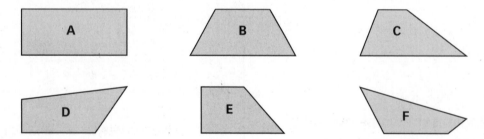

Choose a partner and read the clues for one of your figures out loud. Does your partner's drawing match the figure you chose? Explain how the figures can be different, even if your partner did not make a mistake.

Reflect on Mathematical Practices

After you complete the task, choose one of the following questions to answer.

1. **Be Precise** List all of the geometry words you used to write your clues that describe your figures. What do these words mean?

2. **Use Tools** What tools could you use to make accurate drawings of your figures? Why would you need each of these tools?

©Curriculum Associates, LLC   Copying is not permitted.

Common Core State Standards for Mathematics, Grade 3

The chart below correlates each Common Core State Standard to the *Ready® Common Core Instruction* lesson(s) that offer(s) comprehensive instruction on that standard. Use this chart to determine which lessons your students should complete based on their mastery of each standard.

Common Core State Standards for Grade 3 — Mathematics Standards		Content Emphasis	*Ready® Common Core Instruction* Lesson(s)
Operations and Algebraic Thinking			
Represent and solve problems involving multiplication and division.			
3.OA.A.1	Interpret products of whole numbers, e.g., interpret 5 × 7 as the total number of objects in 5 groups of 7 objects each. *For example, describe a context in which a total number of objects can be expressed as 5 × 7.*	Major	1
3.OA.A.2	Interpret whole-number quotients of whole numbers, e.g., interpret 56 ÷ 8 as the number of objects in each share when 56 objects are partitioned equally into 8 shares, or as a number of shares when 56 objects are partitioned into equal shares of 8 objects each. *For example, describe a context in which a number of shares or a number of groups can be expressed as 56 ÷ 8.*	Major	4
3.OA.A.3	Use multiplication and division within 100 to solve word problems in situations involving equal groups, arrays, and measurement quantities, e.g., by using drawings and equations with a symbol for the unknown number to represent the problem.	Major	11
3.OA.A.4	Determine the unknown whole number in a multiplication or division equation relating three whole numbers. *For example, determine the unknown number that makes the equation true in each of the equations 8 × ? = 48, 5 = __ ÷ 3, 6 × 6 = ?*	Major	6
Understand properties of multiplication and the relationship between multiplication and division.			
3.OA.B.5	Apply properties of operations as strategies to multiply and divide. *Examples: If 6 × 4 = 24 is known, then 4 × 6 = 24 is also known. (Commutative property of multiplication.) 3 × 5 × 2 can be found by 3 × 5 = 15, then 15 × 2 = 30, or by 5 × 2 = 10, then 3 × 10 = 30. (Associative property of multiplication.) Knowing that 8 × 5 = 40 and 8 × 2 = 16, one can find 8 × 7 as 8 × (5 + 2) = (8 × 5) + (8 × 2) = 40 + 16 = 56. (Distributive property.)*	Major	2, 3
3.OA.B.6	Understand division as an unknown-factor problem. *For example, find 32 ÷ 8 by finding the number that makes 32 when multiplied by 8.*	Major	5
Multiply and divide within 100.			
3.OA.C.7	Fluently multiply and divide within 100, using strategies such as the relationship between multiplication and division (e.g., knowing that 8 × 5 = 40, one knows 40 ÷ 5 = 8) or properties of operations. By the end of Grade 3, know from memory all products of two one-digit numbers.	Major	6
Solve problems involving the four operations, and identify and explain patterns in arithmetic.			
3.OA.D.8	Solve two-step word problems using the four operations. Represent these problems using equations with a letter standing for the unknown quantity. Assess the reasonableness of answers using mental computation and estimation strategies including rounding.	Major	12, 13
3.OA.D.9	Identify arithmetic patterns (including patterns in the addition table or multiplication table), and explain them using properties of operations. *For example, observe that 4 times a number is always even, and explain why 4 times a number can be decomposed into two equal addends.*	Major	7

The Standards for Mathematical Practice are integrated throughout the instructional lessons.

© Copyright 2013. National Governors Association Center for Best Practices and Council of Chief State School Officers. All rights reserved.

©Curriculum Associates, LLC   Copying is not permitted.

Common Core State Standards for Grade 3 — Mathematics Standards	Content Emphasis	Ready® Common Core Instruction Lesson(s)
Number and Operations in Base Ten		
Use place value understanding and properties of operations to perform multi-digit arithmetic.		
3.NBT.A.1 Use place value understanding to round whole numbers to the nearest 10 or 100.	Supporting/ Additional	8
3.NBT.A.2 Fluently add and subtract within 1000 using strategies and algorithms based on place value, properties of operations, and/or the relationship between addition and subtraction.	Supporting/ Additional	9
3.NBT.A.3 Multiply one-digit whole numbers by multiples of 10 in the range 10–90 (e.g., 9×80, 5×60) using strategies based on place value and properties of operations.	Supporting/ Additional	10
Number and Operations—Fractions		
Develop understanding of fractions as numbers.		
3.NF.A.1 Understand a fraction $\frac{1}{b}$ as the quantity formed by 1 part when a whole is partitioned into b equal parts; understand a fraction $\frac{a}{b}$ as the quantity formed by a parts of size $\frac{1}{b}$.	Major	14
3.NF.A.2 Understand a fraction as a number on the number line; represent fractions on a number line diagram.	Major	15
3.NF.A.2a Represent a fraction $\frac{1}{b}$ on a number line diagram by defining the interval from 0 to 1 as the whole and partitioning it into b equal parts. Recognize that each part has size $\frac{1}{b}$ and that the endpoint of the part based at 0 locates the number $\frac{1}{b}$ on the number line.	Major	15
3.NF.A.2b Represent a fraction $\frac{a}{b}$ on a number line diagram by marking off a lengths $\frac{1}{b}$ from 0. Recognize that the resulting interval has size $\frac{a}{b}$ and that its endpoint locates the number $\frac{a}{b}$ on the number line.	Major	15
3.NF.A.3 Explain equivalence of fractions in special cases, and compare fractions by reasoning about their size.	Major	16, 17, 18, 19
3.NF.A.3a Understand two fractions as equivalent (equal) if they are the same size, or the same point on a number line.	Major	16
3.NF.A.3b Recognize and generate simple equivalent fractions, e.g., $\frac{1}{2} = \frac{2}{4}$, $\frac{4}{6} = \frac{2}{3}$. Explain why the fractions are equivalent, e.g., by using a visual fraction model.	Major	17
3.NF.A.3c Express whole numbers as fractions, and recognize fractions that are equivalent to whole numbers. Examples: *Express 3 in the form* $3 = \frac{3}{1}$; *recognize that* $\frac{6}{1} = 6$; *locate* $\frac{4}{4}$ *and 1 at the same point of a number line diagram.*	Major	17
3.NF.A.3d Compare two fractions with the same numerator or the same denominator by reasoning about their size. Recognize that comparisons are valid only when the two fractions refer to the same whole. Record the results of comparisons with the symbols $>$, $=$, or $<$, and justify the conclusions, e.g., by using a visual fraction model.	Major	18, 19
Measurement and Data		
Solve problems involving measurement and estimation.		
3.MD.A.1 Tell and write time to the nearest minute and measure time intervals in minutes. Solve word problems involving addition and subtraction of time intervals in minutes, e.g., by representing the problem on a number line diagram.	Major	20, 21
3.MD.A.2 Measure and estimate liquid volumes and masses of objects using standard units of grams (g), kilograms (kg), and liters (l). Add, subtract, multiply, or divide to solve one-step word problems involving masses or volumes that are given in the same units, e.g., by using drawings (such as a beaker with a measurement scale) to represent the problem.	Major	22, 23

The Standards for Mathematical Practice are integrated throughout the instructional lessons.

©Curriculum Associates, LLC   Copying is not permitted.

Common Core State Standards for Grade 3 — Mathematics Standards	Content Emphasis	Ready® Common Core Instruction Lesson(s)
Measurement and Data (continued)		
Represent and interpret data.		
3.MD.B.3 Draw a scaled picture graph and a scaled bar graph to represent a data set with several categories. Solve one- and two-step "how many more" and "how many less" problems using information presented in scaled bar graphs. *For example, draw a bar graph in which each square in the bar graph might represent 5 pets.*	Supporting/ Additional	24, 25
3.MD.B.4 Generate measurement data by measuring lengths using rulers marked with halves and fourths of an inch. Show the data by making a line plot, where the horizontal scale is marked off in appropriate units—whole numbers, halves, or quarters.	Supporting/ Additional	26
Geometric measurement: understand concepts of area and relate area to multiplication and to addition.		
3.MD.C.5 Recognize area as an attribute of plane figures and understand concepts of area measurement.	Major	27
3.MD.C.5a A square with side length 1 unit, called "a unit square," is said to have "one square unit" of area, and can be used to measure area.	Major	27
3.MD.C.5b A plane figure which can be covered without gaps or overlaps by n unit squares is said to have an area of n square units.	Major	27
3.MD.C.6 Measure areas by counting unit squares (square cm, square m, square in, square ft, and improvised units).	Major	27
3.MD.C.7 Relate area to the operations of multiplication and addition.	Major	28, 29
3.MD.C.7a Find the area of a rectangle with whole-number side lengths by tiling it, and show that the area is the same as would be found by multiplying the side lengths.	Major	28
3.MD.C.7b Multiply side lengths to find areas of rectangles with whole-number side lengths in the context of solving real world and mathematical problems, and represent whole-number products as rectangular areas in mathematical reasoning.	Major	28
3.MD.C.7c Use tiling to show in a concrete case that the area of a rectangle with whole-number side lengths a and $b + c$ is the sum of $a \times b$ and $a \times c$. Use area models to represent the distributive property in mathematical reasoning.	Major	29
3.MD.C.7d Recognize area as additive. Find areas of rectilinear figures by decomposing them into non-overlapping rectangles and adding the areas of the non-overlapping parts, applying this technique to solve real world problems.	Major	29
Geometric measurement: recognize perimeter.		
3.MD.D.8 Solve real world and mathematical problems involving perimeters of polygons, including finding the perimeter given the side lengths, finding an unknown side length, and exhibiting rectangles with the same perimeter and different areas or with the same area and different perimeters.	Supporting/ Additional	30
Geometry		
Reason with shapes and their attributes.		
3.G.A.1 Understand that shapes in different categories (e.g., rhombuses, rectangles, and others) may share attributes (e.g., having four sides), and that the shared attributes can define a larger category (e.g., quadrilaterals). Recognize rhombuses, rectangles, and squares as examples of quadrilaterals, and draw examples of quadrilaterals that do not belong to any of these subcategories.	Supporting/ Additional	31, 32
3.G.A.2 Partition shapes into parts with equal areas. Express the area of each part as a unit fraction of the whole. *For example, partition a shape into 4 parts with equal area, and describe the area of each part as $\frac{1}{4}$ of the area of the shape.*	Supporting/ Additional	33

The Standards for Mathematical Practice are integrated throughout the instructional lessons.

©Curriculum Associates, LLC   Copying is not permitted.